Ready, Tech, Go!

The Definitive Guide to Exporting Australian Technology to Europe

Christelle Damiens

Published in Australia in 2016 by Christelle Damiens

Email: readytechgo@exportia.com.au
Web: www.readytechgo.biz

National Library of Australia Cataloguing-in-Publication entry:

Damiens, Christelle – author.
Ready, Tech, Go! : the definitive guide to exporting Australian technology to Europe / Christelle Damiens.

9780994227706 (paperback)

Small business – Technological innovations – Australia –
Popular works
High technology industries – Australia – Popular works
Export marketing – Europe – Popular works
International trade – Popular works

658.8

Disclaimer

The author has made every effort to ensure the accuracy of the information within this book was correct at the time of publication. The author does not assume and hereby disclaims any liability to any party for any loss, damage or disruption caused by errors or omissions, whether such errors or omissions result from accident, negligence, or any other cause.

Edited by Epiphany Editing & Publishing
Cover design by Boxer and Co
Typesetting by Epiphany Editing and Publishing

CONTENTS

ACKNOWLEDGEMENTS

Grand merci:

A ma cacahuète Maya pour sa patience pendant les longues heures d'écriture.

A mon compagnon Nikolas pour son soutien inconditionnel.

A mes parents et à mon frère, qui m'ont toujours soutenue dans mes pérégrinations.

Aux grands voyageurs chers à mon coeur, Jacques et Sabine qui m'ont insufflé le goût du long cours.

Warm thanks:

To the South Australian community, which welcomed me as a migrant from France from 2006 till 2012; it turned out to be the best choice of location for launching my business, Exportia. I am very grateful to Lyn Hay, Kristine Peters, Cath Duncan, Gordon Thomson, Gordon Kay and Dr Christine Rothauser. Also, to my friends Teresa Golin and Jaqueline Barmentloo for their support and friendship.

To all my clients and partners at Exportia with whom I have been on a journey for the past ten years. Particularly, I would like to thank Dr Alex Birrell, Dale Coleman, Anthony Kittel and Vincent de Sutter. They have challenged me as much as I do them and it has been a very rewarding experience for all concerned!

To Glen Carlson and the Key Person of Influence program. Thank you so much Andrew Griffiths – without you I would not have attempted the adventure of becoming an author. Thank you also to Gwen Blake (book cover design) and Kirsty Ogden (editing and typesetting) for their sound advice and professionalism.

To my team at Exportia for their encouragement and enthusiasm during the progress of 'the book project'. It's been great fun!

PREFACE

In 2006, I migrated from France to Australia. At the time, I worked for IBM in Paris as a sales representative for a large French bank. I found it a great corporate experience and one that I thoroughly enjoyed. Prior to that position, I'd worked for a small business as their export manager. In this role, I reported directly to the CEO and was able to immediately see the results of my work being produced at the factory. I used to travel throughout Europe to develop their retail network – particularly in Germany which was my main market.

With my background in sales, working for both a multinational and a small business, I soon discovered what I enjoyed most. I realised that working for a small business, where you can really make a difference and clearly see direct results, was my real passion. It was definitely an area in which I wanted to be involved in the future.

So, when I made the decision to move to Australia, I initially wondered what I had to offer and how I could use my skills and knowledge to best advantage. It soon became clear that my European business development experience was my strength and I was motivated to work with small businesses again. I consulted IBM and they agreed to give me extended leave in order to pursue opportunities in Australia.

When I migrated to Australia, I did not know anyone or have any local business contacts. I launched my company, Exportia, based simply on my knowledge and expertise of

European business practices and principles, and with faith that I would succeed. I had to gradually build my services and products with quite a lot of trial and error along the way. But I enjoyed every aspect of it and I still love each step of this exciting journey, working with Australian small businesses in Europe.

While working with Australian CEOs of small and medium-sized high-tech businesses over the past nine years, I have experienced moments of joy and success, as well as periods of frustration and exasperation. Commonly, I found that these businesses always seemed to have the same misconceptions and make the same exporting mistakes: they are insufficiently prepared to launch an international venture; have no clear focus on where to take the company internationally; and most importantly, don't have the necessary perseverance to achieve exporting success because they give up too quickly when things get tough.

As my business developed and grew, I became aware that we were able to help Australian companies become successful exporters to Europe by following the same process, over and over again. As a result, I created a comprehensive business exporting program based on a 7-step methodology to support clients through every stage of exporting. My 7-step process (called the 'GoToEurope program') covers each step (or milestone) in the exporting process: Country, Product, Marketing, Channels, Team, Customers, and Forecast and Planning.

This unique exporting program has been designed specifically for tech businesses to lower the risk of failure and to rapidly accelerate sales in Europe. If you are a business owner or manager who currently operates within the high-tech industry, it is my sincere desire that reading this book will help you to achieve success in the highly competitive European market.

Christelle Damiens

INTRODUCTION

···

I f you've made the decision to read this book, it's quite likely that you're the owner or manager of a successful Australian technology business. You love your product and know it could be a valuable resource for an even wider audience. But you're not sure what to do to launch it into the international market or how you can achieve profitability for your organisation through exporting.

A lot of small businesses dream of going global. The internet offers the perception that this is possible and easy to do. At the same time, businesses may get online enquiries via their website from different parts of the world without having the capability or necessary expertise to assess who it is they are actually talking to on the other side of the planet.

Small high-tech companies with ambitious growth objectives understand how important it is to avoid the dependence on their local market in order to mitigate risk in their business. They recognise that diversifying their market presence will result in improved outcomes for their business and greater opportunities for success.

A research study conducted by Deloitte titled, *The Future of Productivity: Smart Exporting for Canadian Companies* indicates that the survival rate of companies which export to international markets compared to those companies which do not currently export is as follows:

- Canada: manufacturing exporters have 69 per cent lower exit rates
- United Kingdom: companies are 11 per cent less likely to shut down if they export
- France: probability of failure falls by 57 per cent after companies start exporting
- India: IT companies that export survive 26 per cent longer.

For this reason, businesses need to grow and expand their interests to international markets to ensure their long-term survival. If we take the example of advanced manufacturing: how can Australian companies lower their manufacturing costs by only relying on the volume of their domestic market? How do they remain competitive in a global market when they are competing with Europeans, Americans, Japanese or Chinese companies which all have very large domestic markets? The enlightened response to these questions is that they have to be prepared to export.

Exporting offers companies both opportunity and risk. So, while it is critical for many businesses to launch into exporting to international markets, at the same time, it is vital to do it the right way.

The subject of exporting can be very overwhelming and many companies looking to export are aware that it can put their business at risk. The common questions small business owners ask when they want to grow their business by exporting internationally is: 'Where do I start?' and 'How do I do it?' Responding to these types of questions is my objective in this book and I'm sure that you'll find that many of your concerns will be addressed as you read through each chapter.

Throughout this book, my main focus is on small-to-medium-sized high-technological businesses that are primarily involved in the information technology, digital and telecommunications industries, the electronics sector, the medical device and health technologies sector, clean environmental technologies, and, more broadly, companies in advanced manufacturing. While I do briefly mention some companies that sell to consumers as well as businesses, for the most part I mainly concentrate on companies dealing with business-to-business transactions and also on industrial applications. The reason is that this is an area where most of my business exporting experience lies and where I can share real-life examples of businesses I have helped to achieve successful outcomes as a result of exporting to international (and, in particular, European) markets. Furthermore, the sales cycle and the structure of the distribution process are quite different for consumer goods where distributors are mainly large retailers, supermarkets and hypermarkets.

This book consists of five sections which are designed to give you an overview of the critical steps necessary in order to successfully compete in the European market. In the first section (*Becoming an Exporter to Europe*), I introduce the exporting consultation process with an evaluation phase to assess your business model and your suitability to becoming an exporter. In the second section (*Identifying your Reasons for Exporting to Europe*), I then make sure you are really clear on why you want to export to the European market. The third section (*Starting your European Enterprise on the Right Foot*) covers the critical preparation required to become a successful exporter. The fourth section (*All Systems Go!*) is where you start to get the ball rolling; it is all about how you approach your future European clients. The last section (*Achieving Sustainable Export Sales*) is very important and is where I explain how to secure long-term business success in Europe. Often the first sales can be easy, but it is only by correctly following this last step that you can really take your business to the next level.

Background Information about the European Union

As at 1st January, 2014, the European Union represents a population of 507 million people. At this point in time there were 24 official languages in the European Union with 56 per cent of European Union citizens speaking another language other than their mother tongue and 28 per cent speaking two additional languages.

So, how does it work? The European Union is an association of 28 European countries that are each run independently. However, they have a common European parliament which establishes laws and regulations that apply to member countries. What does this mean for an exporter from outside the European Union? It means that goods, services and people can circulate from one country to another without customs formalities. The Euro is used in most of the European Union member-countries and is the common currency for trade. However, there are a few remaining exceptions, such as the British Pound and Danish Krone.

If, like most of my clients, you are playing in the high-tech space, I recommend that you consider that Europe could be a good market for you as it has the ability to buy highly innovative technology for a premium price. Of the top 500 Fortune companies, more than one hundred are Western European companies.

SECTION ONE

Becoming an Exporter to Europe

1

Getting Ready to Export to Europe

Before launching your company into the European market it is important for you to question whether or not the timing is right for your business to begin exporting. Do you have all of the necessary resources – both financial and human – that are required for you to become a profitable exporter?

In this chapter, I will cover all of the things you need to check and prepare for to achieve success in the European market. In addition, I will discuss the activities you can do in the preliminary stages of your exporting journey, before even beginning to make contact with potential overseas clients. Remember, you need to be well prepared before you start talking to a potential buyer.

Do You Have a Well-Developed Business Model?

The first very common and basic mistake that many small business owners make is to think that they can start exporting without having fully developed their business model. By this I mean that the company may have not fully developed its local

Australian business but is already looking to try to engage with potential export customers.

When a company is in its formative stages, has not yet worked out how it is going to operate, or it only generates a limited revenue (a few hundred thousand dollars per annum), there is no point in considering the option to export.

Of course, as you will learn while reading this book, it is important to take the needs and wants of international markets into account during the early stages of a business, so research is essential. However, to be already looking for European clients when you haven't worked out what you have to offer your local market may put your business at risk from the outset.

I'm sure this first pitfall may sound very basic to the majority of you. Yet, over the years, quite a few small business owners have come to me seeking my help to start exporting to Europe without having properly developed their Australian business. In such cases, I systematically refuse to actively conduct business development in Europe for them because it puts their business in too much financial risk. The best advice I can offer these companies at this point is an overview of what is happening in the European market within their industry or initial feedback from potential clients. When I meet this type of business owner, I always offer to stay in touch, and I advise them that I can assist them with initial research into the European market.

Understand Your Target Market

Before considering exporting your technology to Europe, it is important for you to have a good understanding of your target market. What I mean by target market is the types of clients to whom your business is particularly relevant. For example, you are able to often close deals in a specific industry because your product or service solves problems they have or is relevant to the industry. In this case, you simply need to define that client profile and use this definition as a starting point for your exporting activities. This is an important exercise because it will save you a lot of time to know that you can easily seek out these clients because you already understand this market and its issues. The exception to this is the situation where a particular industry has quite a low profile in Europe.

Generally speaking, the first criteria that most European customers are going to assess you by are your references from satisfied clients in your local market. You can be certain that serious companies will always take this step. Therefore, if you have not quite worked out who your target market is and which industry sector is clearly your sweet spot, it will be very costly for you to try to figure it out in a foreign market.

In your home market, it is cheaper for you to visit potential local clients and to validate their interest in what you do. In the case of a foreign market (and particularly a European country), it is costly and time consuming to discover who could be your potential customer if you don't already have a clear picture or know who or what you are seeking.

At this point, I should clearly emphasise that small high-tech businesses that have only recently launched will find it much harder to achieve success in the European market. There are various reasons for this. It is important for European customers to feel completely confident that your company is reliable and will not, for example, go bankrupt once they buy your product. Consequently, if you don't have any tangible customers and revenue to prove your business viability, it will be harder to convince any potential new clients. European companies will conduct due diligence on you by quizzing you about who you are currently selling to and why they do business with you. They want to find out whether or not you're a trustworthy company. For example, if you supply your product or service to your home country government, your credibility will instantly rise in the eyes of your potential European customer. It also demonstrates that you have some financial stability.

REAL-WORLD TOOL: Assessing if you are Ready to Export to Europe

In order to develop your understanding of the steps involved in exporting to Europe, I recommend you watch the video, 'Know your Sweet Spot' available on the Exportia Australia YouTube channel

2

Born-global Businesses – Illusion or Reality?

By now, some of you may be thinking (and I have heard my clients ask the question many times before): 'What if my home market is not the ideal market for me?' And this may actually be the case for your business. To give you an example, one of my Australian clients produces software for railways and had clearly identified that his main market would be Europe due to the extensive European railway network for freight and passengers. So, relatively quickly, he established an office in Europe. He still continued to develop his home market with a few key clients and now has a small commercial team looking after them. After having developed a solid Australian base, he was able to invest in an office in the United Kingdom.

You may have also heard of the 'born-global' concept, particularly in relation to the information and communications technology and digital sector. This expression is often used for start-ups that launch their business at the international level.

One of the first questions I usually ask owners of small and medium-sized businesses who want to make the transition to exporting is: 'Do you have the financial means to support an exporting operation in your company in the long term? Are you ready for a close-to-zero return on investment during the first two years?' If you have not developed your local market sufficiently well to support this investment, then exporting can be a risky venture. Of course, there are some exceptions to this as mentioned above. However, if you already have significant financial resources readily available and your investors have patience, then you will be alright.

Nevertheless, for the most part I am quite sceptical about the 'born-global' concept. Yet I do acknowledge that there are a few exceptions. A small number of start-ups achieve global success rapidly when, for example, the management team has a solid international network and experience, and an overseas investor is involved. In this case, contracts with overseas companies are often signed in the first few years of a start-up company's existence. Another exception is digital businesses that require only a low level of interaction with their clients. These types of businesses have fully standardised their online solution and rely solely on online sales – typically Google or Atlassian (the Australian success story). At some stage, these companies require some level of local presence in order to become sustainable in the long term.

Often, small and medium-sized enterprises may conduct an initial market study to determine their viability for exporting to Europe because they think they've reached a point where they're ready to invest in the early phases. However, they often don't realise that these initials steps (i.e. market study, market evaluation, etc.) are the cheapest ones and the next steps are much more expensive (i.e. regular visits, local presence, local technical support, etc.). Therefore, before attempting to dip your toe in the waters of the global marketplace, it's a good idea to make sure that your business financials are healthy. If your turnover is below one million $US/AUD you are potentially putting your business at risk if you want to venture into exporting, because sales aren't likely to occur instantly.

EXAMPLE CASE STUDY: Exploring Opportunities to Export to Germany

To illustrate my point about the costs involved in exporting, here is a quick example:

Let's assume you are a high-tech business with an annual turnover of $US500,000 and you decide you'd like to explore opportunities in the German market. What kind of expenses can you reasonably expect when you're starting out as an exporter?

Table 1 has been created as a rough guide to help you assess initial costs when venturing into exporting. It outlines what, in my opinion, are the minimum expenses involved in the initial stages of launching your business into the European market.

First, you will need to commission a bespoke market study (at a cost of 5,000 Euros) to see if your product has some traction in the European market and to help you to identify the main distributors. Before contacting them, you realise it would be a good idea to have a one-page brochure about your company printed in German (500 Euros) because Germany seems to be a good market for your business. Next, after contacting a couple of German distributors, you decide that you will need to meet them (five-day trip to Germany, 5,000 Euros minimum in travel expenses, plus the cost of a return flight to your home country). The distributor you meet is likely to ask you if you could translate your manuals into German (1,500 Euros – depending on the size of the document). If you are lucky and one of the distributors you met during your German visit agrees to distribute your product within a few months, there will be further costs involved. For example, this distributor may attend an annual trade show in September. He requests that you help them with their next trade show in order to launch your product. You then decide that it would be worthwhile sending some brochures to them and that, on this occasion, you should probably travel to Germany again. You need to allocate additional funds to print brochures. Plus, you will have one more overseas trip, so you need to plan for the associated costs. It may be useful for you to bring some free 'goodies' as well. You are also aware that you will need to ship some samples for demonstration purposes. So, probably the total cost for you to attend this trade show would be between 5,000 and 10,000 Euros minimum.

This very basic cost analysis exercise assumes you already have your product certified for the European market. If you don't, you will have to make allowance for this expense as well.

TABLE 1: Breakdown of initial export costs associated with the first year of exporting activities in one country (e.g. Germany)

ACTIVITY	MINIMUM COST IN EUROS	MULTIPLIER
Initial market study	5,000	Number of European countries covered
	5,000	
Identifying and contacting distributors (engaging a consultant)	5,000 – 12,000	Size of project
One-page bro-chure	500	Design work Translation costs depends on number of words
Return flight to Germany	1,000	Home country distance from Europe
Meeting in Germany	5,000	Travel costs dependent on duration and number of meetings
Translation into German of a user manual	2,500	Number of words in manuals/Number of manuals
	14,000 – 21,000	

ACTIVITY	MINIMUM COST IN EUROS	MULTIPLIER
Printing 500 brochures and shipping to the distributor	700	Shipping costs: 500 Euros is a bare minimum
Return flight to Germany	1,000	Home country distance from Europe
Cost of stay for trade show (5 days)	2,000	Cost of hotel rooms in Germany during trade show can be very expensive
Banner	500	Printing and shipping costs
Goodies	250	Shipping costs
Samples	500	Cost of products Shipping costs
	4,950	
TOTAL MINIMUM YEAR 1 IN EUROS	23,950 – 30,950	

This total amount of approximately 25,000 Euros is applicable only for the first year of operation as an exporter to only one European country (and I'm being very conservative here). It's quite likely that you will double that cost during the second year of export operations (e.g. more visits, more advertising, etc.).

3

Positioning Your Business in Europe

When I started my export consultancy, Exportia, I did a lot of cold calling in order to find potential clients who were looking to sell their product to the European market. Occasionally, I would come across a small business owner who would claim that their product was so unique there was nothing else like it globally and that it would have huge success in the European market. Of course, this claim would always instantly trigger my interest. And when I'm interested, I usually delve further by asking the following questions: 'So, how did you research your competition? How different is your product? Do you have any patents for it?' What I'm seeking from them is a response such as: 'Our competitors are XYZ, and our differentiator is that we have this specific system that makes our product much xxx-er so buyers switch to us because they can't get this in another product. We have a patent on this system. We respond to a common problem in our industry, which is ... and our competitors don't.'

Identifying Your Competition

Obviously, if you are not aware of what your competitors are doing in their businesses, you need to quickly take steps to find out. In any business venture there is always competition – even indirect competition in that your potential client will compare your product against others. To give you an example, a software developer's indirect competition involves his client using internal programmers instead of hiring an external developer. The direct competition will be other software developers. Another example in the machinery field would be that of using a manual process rather than using your machine to produce the desired outcome. You need then to be able to explain how your machine is going to benefit the business compared to having a worker manually doing the job.

For a small business looking at expanding into Europe, the best way to gain interesting insights is to conduct in-depth research about your European competitors. What you are trying to do here is identify who your major competitors are: they may be European companies or US companies that are well established in Europe. As a guide, I suggest that you pick your top three to five products and find the equivalent items in several European countries. You can focus first on the three major European economies: Germany, UK and France. Of course, if you already have some market information indicating that another country has potential for your product or service, then add it to your list. If you don't know any French or German, get some external assistance to help you overcome the language barriers and to gain an insight into their positioning. Again, you need to determine several criteria that are relevant to your product or service: they could be such things as performance, design, ease of use, warranty, price point, or customer support. Generally speaking, European products will have a multilingual user manual available online. It is a great way to cut through their marketing message and check what the product is really like. The objective is for you to identify your edge in the European market. By doing this research, you should gain a feel for how your products or services compare to those of your competitors. It is also an interesting exercise to check out your competitors' sizes.

Once you have a feel for how your product compares with the competition, you should ask yourself: 'Do I stand a chance with my product in this market? Do I have a lot of competitors or only a few? Are my differentiators strong enough to create an interest in the market?'

If you think at this stage that the competition in Europe seems to be too intense and you're not clear on the 'value-add' that your product or service has in comparison with European competitors, then it is a good idea to get some help from your technical team and share your findings with them. Could they take this market information into account for any future product releases? Get some help from them to really qualify the current competition's product and to identify your strengths. I recommend buying some of these competitor products. Have a look at options available online. I sometimes do this for our clients through my French-based business.

On the other hand, if you think you do have an edge – your product has specific features that have a real 'value-add' for your potential European buyers, and clients from your home market have already indicated their willingness to buy your product over your competitors' products – then you are in a good position to start preparing for export markets.

Drilling Down to Find Your Ideal European Market

One important factor to determine when you have European competitors for your product or service is which European country they come from? Keep that information in mind; it will be important when it comes to selecting which country you should start exporting to. For example, you came across a major player in your industry that is German and extremely well established. You find out down the track that Germany is one of your major target markets. Do you necessarily start by exporting to Germany?

The other important factor at this stage is to find out in which European markets your competitors are most active. Checking out your competitors' websites is key: who do they refer their clients to in Italy, Germany, Belgium, Sweden, Spain, etc.? In some countries, they will only refer to their head office; in other countries they will have a distributor or they will refer you to their local subsidiary. Basically, if your competition has invested in a presence in the UK, Benelux (Belgium, Netherlands, Luxemburg) and/or Scandinavia – but not in Italy, Spain and France – then they are probably targeting an industry that is important there. Maybe it is their historical geographical footprint and their neighbouring markets. This basic analysis will give you some hints as to which country you should start exporting to first. Your ultimate goal is to find a country where you have as little competition as possible and the biggest potential market.

The next step is for you to analyse your competitors' distribution channels. You need to look for such information as: have they established a company in these three markets? Do they use an importer or distributors? What is the profile of these distributors? Do they have agents? Do they sell directly online or not?

Why is this such an important step to take before venturing into an export market? What you need to understand is that buying from another country is a hurdle for your potential client, particularly as you don't already come from the European Union. So for your client to switch to your product, the incentive is going to have to be significant and if you can't articulate it clearly to your potential buyer, they won't buy from you.

Looking After Your Export Clients

When a European client is buying from an overseas company, their main fear is that they will see your company once and then never see it again. What we need to be conscious of is that, in sales, it is usually the person who makes the decision to buy a specific product who is going to be held responsible if anything goes wrong. So, for a European company buying from overseas or from a non-European supplier, a decision to buy your 'foreign' product is perceived as being a higher risk for them. If anything goes wrong with your product, they can't just call you in immediately to get things fixed. Consequently, that person or that small team are actually being quite brave making the decision to buy your product. So, what can you do to make your buyer feel he or she is making a good decision and not taking a risk when buying your product?

Initially, you need to make them feel that you will be there for them – it is really that simple. As a bare minimum, you need to visit them regularly (not just once or twice a year), so that you have the opportunity to create trust with your client and to make them feel as though they are supported and important to you.

REAL-WORLD TOOL: Survey – Compiling an Initial List of Potential European Customers

This survey is designed to help you to develop a better understanding of those countries that may be potential markets for your exporting activities, as well as those countries that appear to be fairly competitive (refer to Table 2 below). At this stage, I suggest that you don't attach too much importance to these countries; they should be considered simply as initial market intelligence.

TABLE 2: Survey to Compile an Initial List of Potential European Clients

	COUNTRIES
Have you ever had an enquiry from any European customers? If so, from which country(ies)?	
Have you ever had an enquiry from any European distributors? If so, from which country(ies)?	
Do you regularly have any European visitors to your website? Check Google Analytics to find their country of origin.	
Are any of your domestic market competitors present in Europe? If yes, in which countries do they sell?	

	COUNTRIES
Where are your European competitors' headquarters located?	
Competitor 1	
Competitor 2	
Competitor 3	
Xxx	
In which European countries do your competitors have a subsidiary?	
Competitor 1	
Competitor 2	
Competitor 3	
Xxx	
In which European countries do your competitors have distributors?	
Competitor 1	
Competitor 2	
Competitor 3	
Xxx	
Countries which seem to offer potential	
Countries which seem to be fairly competitive	

4

Your Product – Is it Appropriate for a Global Market?

One of the critical things you need to do before becoming an exporter is to assess your chances of being successful, including defining whether your product has a unique place in the market and if it can add any value for your potential clients.

Being unique would seem to be great in itself. But what if you have a unique product that is useless to your target market? I'll give you an example to illustrate my point. One of my previous clients had a highly skilled and resourceful Research and Development team. Being very experienced engineers, they had designed an exciting new product. The product features were very innovative and unique, and were designed to provide a lot of technical information to the end-user. However, this product was clearly conceived by engineers and it would have been useful if other engineers were the clients who'd be using it, because it was so complex. Can you imagine what actually happened when we tried to sell this product internationally to a target market that mainly consisted of retirees with an average

age of 65 years? They were scared to buy the product because it had too many associated functions and features. The resellers were scared to sell it to their clients because they thought: 'If I install this product, my clients are going to call me all the time wanting explanations on how to use it.' And they also thought it was going to be much too difficult to sell. The product itself was the most advanced in the market and had many unique features, yet it did not fit the needs of the target market.

What can you do to avoid this situation? First of all, use your home market to test the uniqueness of your product. Since we live in a globalised world, the competitors like those you find in your home country will also exist in Europe. Maybe not all of them, but it will still be a good place to begin checking what they're doing. So, study the competitive products in your home market very closely. You need to compare the features of your product/service with those of your competitors'. I suspect if you have been in business for a while, you would already know who they are. I recommend that you check your competitors' products in a matrix and conduct a feature comparison survey. For example, for a technical product, usage comparison points could include: performance (e.g. power, autonomy, speed), design features (e.g. size, weight, portability), ease of use (e.g. user-friendliness, customer interface), warranty, price point and customer support (e.g. YouTube training videos, 24/7 support line).

What could be even more interesting would be to do this exercise with a European competitor who is active in your home country. This will give you a lot of valuable information to use when you are ready to start targeting the European market. Since the situation can change very rapidly, with new products regularly coming onto the market, I suggest that you regularly update this matrix.

Leveraging Existing European Contacts

An easy task at this stage of your export planning strategy is to ask your team if they have previously fielded any enquiries from the European market and from which country or countries. Are they recent? Have they stopped for any reason? Who are these European contacts? I recommend you interview them to find out more information and to learn what you can do to increase your chances of exporting success.

Here is a quick sample interview with a fictitious Spanish client: 'I would like to thank you for buying from us. We would really value your feedback about our product to better understand how we could provide you with improved service as we are planning to increase our presence in the European market. I have a couple of questions – are you happy to answer them now?

'Can you please tell me more about your industry? What is the size of your company? How do you use our product? How did you find out about us? Why did you buy from us? What feedback can you give us about our product? Which product do you usually buy? Where do you buy it? If you wanted to buy our product in Spain, who would you like to buy it from? Which distributor do you think would do an excellent job? Thank you very much for taking the time to respond to me. Would it be okay if I contact you again in a few months, as we are currently working through our export strategy for Europe?'

You will be amazed how customers love to be interviewed! They are a gold mine of information for you, particularly if they feel that you value them. Don't only rely on their feedback; however, they can be a great source to check facts and obtain other information. Keep a record of this information for future use.

Compliance and Relevance to the European Market

To sell your product in the European market, it must be manufactured with a European audience in mind. It is a costly mistake to design a product that does not fit with the standards and needs of European clients. If you do, it obviously makes it hard (if not impossible) to sell your product to them.

One day, while I was at the airport about to board a flight to Germany, I got a phone call from one of my Exportia team members saying the export manager from a client company had called to ask if her product needed to comply with the European standards. It seemed to be quite urgent, so I called the person back. They were already selling to the European market and they wanted to check if they had to comply with any specific standards. From that point, I had alarm bells ringing. Of course you first need to check if your product will comply to a country's specifications before you attempt to sell it. You should even plan for it during the product's design phase.

Sometimes, differentiations may lie in the fact that you are a newcomer and the market wants novelty. However, this novelty factor needs to be backed up by more substantial differentiating factors to be able to sustain clients' interest over the long term.

What can you do if you find that your European competitors are well ahead of you? Does that mean that the European market has needs which are different from those of your home market? Or does it mean that you need to play catch-up?

At one stage, I had a prime viewpoint of the European competition within the automotive market and shared it with my client. He was then in a very good position to identify some of these European companies which were entering his own home market. This was definitely an asset when he was able to explain to his own client (who was being offered the European solution) that he was aware of the European solution and that it was known to be a low-end, cut-rate product. He could then more easily justify his premium and reliability positioning. In this way, exporting can also help small businesses in their home market – an amazing side benefit!

5

Exporting Challenges for Small Businesses

Starting an export business is a challenging process and can gobble up an essential resource of small business owners – time. A situation I commonly observe is a small business owner attempting to manage the home market and the export market at the same time. While it is good for the business owner to have a feel for what is occurring in the European market, it's important that they do not spread their attention and resources too wide. For example, the small business owner may decide to go on a business trip to Europe for a minimum of ten days to visit a trade show. During this visit, she meets with about ten to twenty European companies. On her return to Australia, she has to urgently solve a couple of issues with her teams, and so on. As a result, there is no time for follow-ups with her European contacts and all of the relevant information is lost. The company then loses momentum because the small business owner is slow to get the information to overseas clients and, consequently, the leads go cold.

An Unengaged Team

A year ago, I was feeling quite frustrated with one of my clients – a small business in the electronics sector. I was involved in helping this company export to several European markets and, in particular, I was developing a lot of leads for them in the French market. The momentum was building up slowly, year by year. But I always experienced a very slow response from my client's team to any of my queries. They took a long time to get back to me when I had to provide information to a European customer. A typical response from them was: 'I have this and this that I have been asked to do, so I won't have time before the end of the week.' In short, all of my enquiries were treated as the last priority by everyone in the team, even though the CEO in this business had very ambitious export development goals. As is my usual response when I don't get the desired outcome for my clients, I called the CEO to voice my frustration that we were clearly losing momentum with the European clients. When we discussed the situation, we realised that his team was not sufficiently engaged in the export project. They always gave priority to their home market and, in this respect, they were clearly doing their job. There is nothing wrong with that; they just weren't aligned with the strategic objectives of the company. As a result of that conversation, we got his management committee together and pointed out the roadblocks to them. They clearly identified the problems and realised they had not integrated exporting operations into their daily work processes. After this meeting, the mindset of the whole team changed.

6

Intellectual Property Protection and Compliance

The majority of my clients are technology companies and they often own the intellectual property on their product. This means that in sectors such as advanced manufacturing they frequently commence the research and development stage many years before the actual commercialisation of the product. In addition, planning for compliance to European regulations and standards is of paramount importance within technology sectors.

Protecting Your Intellectual Property

I have to say that, for the most part, European Union members are quite respectful of intellectual property (IP). To give you an example, two years ago I exhibited at a trade show in Frankfurt. The organisation responsible for hosting the trade show was Messe Frankfurt and they conducted a campaign during the event: 'Messe Frankfurt against copying'. The soft approach to the campaign involved promotional stands to raise awareness about the issue and dissuade intellectual property thieves. The hard (and dramatic) approach was actual arrests, with the German police shutting down stands where copies of genuine products were found.

There are several methods that IP lawyers can use to help you ensure you have an excellent level of intellectual property protection. If your technology is subject to patent registration, then you will be aware that, during this process, you will need to make some important decisions with respect to patent applications and registrations. You need to review the process with your lawyer, who will ask you which areas of the world you want to protect your IP in and where they should lodge a patent application for you. This is an important recurring investment so it needs to be in line with your export strategy. Another important decision you need to make concerns country selection. You will need to lodge your patent in the selected European countries if you feel these markets are right for you, or for the whole European Union if you can afford it.

Your lawyer can walk you through the process of lodging a Patent Cooperation Treaty (PCT) application rather than a single-country application. This is where your initial market research is important so that you select the right country and are savvy about your budget. Don't forget: there are the initial application lodgement costs, as well as the recurring fees involved in patents.

If your company has filed a patent application, your lawyer would already have conducted a search on your behalf for patents filed for products with some similarities to your product. It's useful if they can share these companies' names with you. They would normally do so, but if not, make sure you ask them to share this information with you.

A few of my past clients made the conscious decision not to register a patent and to keep their invention or processes secret. Similarly, some former clients also used several tricks to make it challenging for other companies to copy their products. For example, a software company I know sub-contracted its software development to different companies in different parts of the world. Interestingly, I discovered that one of my electronics clients was doing the same thing with the parts and components they were assembling in Australia.

It is always a good idea to register trademarks for slogans, product names, logos and brands. Likewise, having a simple non-disclosure agreement prepared is an effective way to protect your intellectual property, particularly if you are in the early developmental stages and gathering feedback about a product. It is usually well accepted within Europe to sign a simple and short non-disclosure agreement and it's okay to provide them in English.

Compliance

At the same time, you will need to make sure that the product you're currently developing complies with the certifications required in your target market. When targeting the European market, ensure that your technical team has studied the European standards for your product. If you don't have that skillset in-house there are a number of consulting firms that can help you. They can identify the right standard for you and offer advice about the different tests your product will need to pass to become certified. This is another expense you will have to budget for. In parallel, what you can do is to check which standards your competition are complying with. More importantly, if you make sure early on that your products are designed to the European standard, you maximise your chances of them passing the tests and you minimise the time spent on this activity.

I have personally been involved in several cases where companies that were already selling to Europe sought our advice to find out if their product needed to comply with the European standard. Generally speaking, technology companies need to have their products certified to the European standard to be able to sell them in Europe. Often the first port of call is to check if the product or solution needs to be CE Marked. So be sure to plan for this process by checking out this requirement early.

What happens if you sell a product that is not certified when it should be? The local safety organisation (for example, a local medical safety authority) will withdraw your product from commercialisation. And you can forget about selling to the European market – your reputation will be completely damaged. Plus, imagine how the people you have already sold your product to will feel about doing business with you in the future.

In some cases, there will be similarities between your home country's and the European Union standards. The certifications process is then much simpler. The other thing is that if you ensure early on that your products comply, you will minimise the risk of your certification process taking a long time and of possibly being unsuccessful. If your product does fail, it means you will have to go through the certification process again – a costly exercise and one that will delay the commercialisation process.

7

Financial Resources and Funding for Exporting Operations

Now that you have almost reached the end of this first section, you will have a better understanding of the research you need to undertake and the budget you will need to plan for before launching into exporting. At this stage, it's important for you to have that yearly figure in mind and for you to feel confident that your business can afford it for two to three years without the benefit of any large export sales. Of course, ideally, you want to generate sales fast, but that will not always happen so you need to be prepared.

A number of government organisations run programs and schemes to encourage small businesses to export. Governments view exporting as an excellent way to create jobs in their local region, state or nation, or in a specific industry. And this view is absolutely correct!

In the preliminary phase (and before committing to any export-related expenses), it is useful to obtain the latest information about government funding for exporting activities. Check what is involved in the application process and if your business could be eligible. You will also need to check the timelines, such as the application submission date and when you can expect to receive the funds. It is also important to determine the way in which the funding scheme works: you need to find out if it is an actual subsidy. In Australia, some government programs, called Export Market Development Grants (EMDG), subsidise up to 50 per cent of your export-related expenses. You need to first spend your export dollar over the period of a year and then lodge your application and receive your subsidy in one annual lump sum.

The other thing to check is what types of expenses are covered, such as marketing, travel or IP-related expenses. Maybe the scheme in your country is completely different from this, in that you don't actually receive a subsidy, but instead receive some form of insurance to cover your expenses if you don't get any sales from these export initiatives.

It is important to do your homework; however, don't rely solely on these government schemes as they can change when governments cut budgets. You should simply consider them as being a nice bonus.

SECTION TWO

Identify Your Reasons for Exporting to Europe

8

Advantages of Exporting to Europe for Your Business

When there are large economic powerhouses like the BRIC (Brazil, Russia, India and China) and the US available to do business with, why should your organisation consider exporting to Europe? This is a very good question to ask as there are many arguments in favour of moving to the European market.

The European Union offers you access to a market of 28 countries and, as of 1 January 2014, represented a population of 507 million people. Of course, just because you sell to one European country doesn't necessarily mean that you'll automatically be in a position to sell to all of them.

If you are like most of my clients and operate within the high-tech space, you will find that Europe is a good market for your business, as it has the capacity to buy highly innovative technology for a premium. Of the top Fortune 500 companies, more than one hundred are Western European companies – the top ones being petrol companies and banks. Most of the countries with the world's highest-purchasing power are located in

Western Europe and many large industrial multinationals (for example, Bayer, Siemens) have their headquarters located there. These multinationals are active around the globe; however, the major decision-making power usually resides within their European headquarters. Even if a European company buys your product outside Europe, it always gives you better leverage and improves your sales and marketing prospects to inform the European headquarters or head-of-division about your products and/or services. Some of my clients have secured contracts with such companies in a number of countries after signing a deal in the multinational's European home country.

Success in European Markets – an Indication of Business Strength

For me, the fact that small and medium-sized Australian companies have been able to export successfully to the European market is concrete proof that their products have real 'value-add'. They have been able to demonstrate that their product or solution is unique and that they have found their market niche. This serves as an indication of long-term success for any small business. Of course, it is never a total surety and it still involves continuous and relentless hard work. Nevertheless, for a small high-tech business, success in Europe is proof that your business is rock-solid. It is my opinion that beyond the obvious benefits of increasing your sales profits, the process of exporting to Europe and all its associated challenges is very valuable for growth for a small business.

On the whole, Europe is quite open to doing business with non-European companies. My clients and I have never suffered rejection because their company was not European. In fact, I have been instrumental in introducing several Australian companies to the European market. According to the *Pocket World in Figures, Edition 2015* (published by the Economist), Germany, Netherlands, France, United Kingdom, Italy and Belgium were among the top fifteen biggest traders of goods in 2013.

Generally speaking, an essential consideration for any small high-tech business is that its products, designs and logos are not copied. In this regard, Europe offers an ideal environment as intellectual property is generally well-respected and valued. Indeed, European countries are very willing to fight for the protection of the intellectual property of their companies. Nevertheless, you should remain on your guard and follow the usual channels to protect your intellectual property.

In the rest of this section, I will discuss such considerations as European Union initiatives and countries' market sizes so that you can develop a better understanding of the situation applicable to your particular industry. This will give you more specific background information to help you decide whether or not to launch your business into exporting to Europe.

9

Research to Define Your Market in Europe

In order to properly prepare for your exporting journey, you need to know how big the opportunity is. Therefore, the initial step is to have a general understanding of the size of the European market for your product. At this point, don't worry too much about choosing a particular country to target your marketing activities. The objective is to gain a broad overview of the whole European market.

There are many ways for you to estimate a market's potential. I'll give you several examples from different industry sectors. The first criteria that usually comes to mind is statistics. Now, how can you easily find statistics about exporting opportunities in Europe? Your first port of call should be all of the European Union web portals; these will provide you with a lot of statistical information for every country in Europe.

It is also useful to check the statistics provided by the professional associations within your industry. I would advise you to identify the German ones as they often provide statistics for the German market, as well as the European market as a whole (and they often supply data for individual European countries).

The reason is that Germans are exporting 'champions' so their industries constantly keep a close watch on their neighbouring export markets. In addition, they usually have market reports available for sale.

The other interesting method to determine whether Europe is a good market for you is to check the European Union initiatives. To give you an example, you may recall me mentioning in Section One about a client who is very active in the railway sector. They'd developed a software program to reduce energy consumption on trains and wanted to break into the European market. In this specific case, I researched to find any European projects underway in that sector which would bring together several European railway operators. I then checked which countries were involved in the project. At this point, I just needed to pull the thread to unravel all the relevant information: which organisation, what division in this organisation, who was the spokesperson? This is usually easy to identify as the project presentations (including the PowerPoint slides or the white paper being presented) are usually online, including the name and (if you are lucky) contact persons. The project presentation will give you some information about the priorities of this organisation. In the case of our railway soft-ware client, they had a very limited number of potential clients in Europe. So, for them, finding statistics wasn't relevant. This is often the case for business to business (B2B) organisations in very niche markets; they may only have a few very large clients. In this situation, you are better off researching market initiatives rather than statistics. For this particular client, we quickly discovered that energy efficiency for railway operators was a priority in the European Union in order to meet the carbon emission reduction targets.

Another of our client examples, which differs in terms of their market research approach, was an automotive equipment manufacturer. This client wanted to find out the size of the

European market in relation to the number of leisure vehicles sold. We located all the statistics we needed from the German leisure vehicles' association website (Caravaning Industrie Verband) which collects all of the European statistics on these types of vehicles. I also found additional data available on the European Union customs web portal when I checked to find out if Europe was importing any leisure vehicles from outside Europe. Our research indicated that Europe was a significant market in terms of leisure vehicles. This information, in turn, prompted my client to design future products to meet European specifications, even though they were not quite ready to export to Europe at that time. As a small business in the B2B space, they were interested in discovering the number of leisure vehicles produced and who manufactured them. So, in this case, we looked for those European industry bodies that represent these manufacturers. These industry bodies collect and share the number of vehicles in circulation, registered and sold – all of the data we required for our research. I can't guarantee you this outcome in 100 per cent of cases, but check the German industry bodies in the first instance. They may well give you an overview of the entire European industry.

10

The Right Attitude for Success

W hen you first commence exporting to Europe, it's important to be aware that you are embarking on a long journey. You need to be willing to invest money and time before getting a return. For this reason, you should always keep the big picture in mind in terms of potential for your business.

You need to have a clear image in mind of why you are going to Europe, as well as the size and opportunity that the European market represents for your business. This will keep you focused when the inevitable difficulties, setbacks and delays occur. It will help you to motivate your team and to be persistent – even when you haven't yet achieved any tangible results.

A key factor that will have a direct influence on your success (or failure) in Europe is having the right attitude. In my own case, I find that I need to tone down some of my small business clients' claims when approaching potential European clients. Ensure that you are not over-confident, but, rather, that you are open to the lessons the European market you're targeting is going to teach you. You need to be aware that these countries are home to very advanced, smart companies that have done business for (sometimes) hundreds of years. Over time, most European businesses have experienced a number of economic crises. I grew up in France and moved to Australia when I was 29 years old. During the period I lived in France, and from the time I was old enough to understand a little bit about economics, I have always been conscious of Europe dealing with economic crisis. Consequently, those businesses that have survived and prospered in spite of economic hardships are very smart and highly efficient. Their organisational structure is streamlined and they manage their costs very tightly. So, always keep this in mind when dealing with European businesses. Of course, the last thing you want is to be perceived as being arrogant (I'm French, so trust me I know what I'm talking about here!).

The Competitive Advantage of Small Businesses

In my exporting business, I find that there are a few rules that are good to observe on my clients' behalf when dealing with the European market. I think the first rule is also relevant for any country with whom you wish to do business; that is, tone it down and be humble. Being a small business within the export market, you need to play to your strengths. The traditional strength of small businesses is that they are agile and customer-focused. You can adapt to your customers' needs faster than any multinational organisation. Your customer service has to be faultless, fast and responsive. Attention to detail and laser-focus on your export clients must be the golden rule in your business. You and I know that, due to their scale, large companies find it very hard to provide high-quality customer service. In contrast, as small business owners, we are in a good position to offer excellent customer service. Your European clients will always be more willing to engage with you if they feel you're actually eager to work with them. You are a small business, so you have to demonstrate that you are going to be there for them.

To give you an example, I have been attempting to sell an innovative Australian electronic product to large French manufacturers in the automotive sector. Over the course of a few years, we attended the same trade show as our French distributor and we visited the same manufacturers. Every year, we delivered the same message to our prospective client: 'We're here for you for the long term. We want to do business with you'. After a few years, we received our first orders from them. And we are currently working with them on their project specifications for their future generation of vehicles. In order for them to trust us and to open up to us about their upcoming plans, they needed to feel confident we were going to be there for them in the long run. It also goes without saying that if you are humble, you will learn a lot from these well-established European companies.

If you are a leader in your home country, use this credential to demonstrate that you are a financially reliable business. Then make it clear to your potential European clients that you are aware the European market is different and you're keen to learn and work with them. Emphasise that you're willing to ensure that your product and/or service meets the specific needs of the European market. You will be surprised – people love it when you ask them for advice and for their feedback.

So, the important lesson here is to ensure that the people on your team you've engaged for your exporting project have the same attitude as you: humility, a willingness to learn, and the ability to provide excellent customer service.

11

Engage Your Entire Team

One key outcome of exporting for small businesses is job creation. By expanding your business into international markets, your team will have more opportunities to grow in their job or to move to a different job. They will also have a better chance of job security. As a business owner, it's also a good opportunity for you to foster staff loyalty. Working for a business which exports around the world also creates a sense of pride for a team.

In my first export manager role for a small French business, I clearly remember that my main objective was to develop their retail network in Europe, and Germany was my first priority. I used to spend one day a week at the office and the rest of the time I'd be out on the road seeking sales opportunities. When the orders started arriving from Germany, the ladies at the factory were delighted. They would come to me and ask who these clients were. This small business had gone through tough economic times and had recently been bought by a larger organisation. It was quite destabilising for the people working in the factory and many of them were fearful about losing their jobs. Seeing orders coming from Germany made them feel confident that the business was headed in the right direction.

Obtain Team Support for the Best Export Results

Naturally, as a small business owner, you are fully committed to the export project. However, you will need the support of your entire team to make it happen. For example, overseas clients will require a fast reply to their technical questions. Consequently, you don't want to have your team saying: 'Who's in charge of this? It's not my responsibility!' You need to have a quick response ready to your client's questions and to have your whole team on board. Likewise, there will be user manuals that will need to be updated into different languages. Your production team must be aware that they have to send a French manual to a French client, or a Europeanised version of your product if you have one. Your marketing team will need to integrate multilingual capability into your website. In addition, regular updating of the German, French and Spanish websites will have to take place.

Basically, for every project you undertake, you need to ask yourself: 'Will this project be relevant for any of our international clients?' To make it a reality, job positions may need to be modified to take on this new international dimension. Ideally, incentives should be given to employees to motivate them to contribute.

Usually, when I conduct a business trip to Europe on behalf of one of our clients, I will, whenever possible, take one of my client's team members with me. Depending on the objective of the trip – whether we are involved in presenting a new product or attending a trade show – either a salesperson or an engineer will come along with me. If the discussion in Europe is going to be very product-oriented, I always find it helpful to take an engineer with me. He or she can then see how the client is currently using the competitors' products. Likewise, they can spot possible technical modifications or improvements that they could add to their product. And, most importantly, they can determine what the engineering team should take on board for their next generation of products and can share this information with the rest of the team back at the office.

Visiting overseas clients is a good way to involve your team. It also makes the requirement of taking into account the needs of international clients more real. Finally, it is a nice reward for your top performers.

As a small business owner, you may have to undertake the initial trips to Europe on your own. In this case, it will be very important to provide feedback to your team on all the information you have gathered during your trip. This feedback should take the form of a trip report and also a debrief meeting. In this way, when you need help conducting the follow-ups after your trip, everybody will understand the context and know what to do.

Communicate Your Export Activities to the Team

One common mistake that I find that many small businesses make is that the owner has a clear vision about taking his business to export markets yet fails to communicate this concept to the rest of the team. There may be a few people working in the business, but they are not aware of what happens in the European markets. This is a major mistake; as a business owner, it is your responsibility to ensure that your organisation learns from all of the relevant information you gather about the European market.

Imagine you're an Australian business and you have an R&D team currently working on the design of a new product. Now imagine Scenario One in which your team develop a new product based on your Australian customers' requirements.

Picture the market potential for this product. Now for Scenario Two, imagine your R&D team is working to satisfy client requirements and specifications from four European countries, as well as from Australia. Which scenario is going to be the most successful in Europe?

If your export activities are disconnected from the rest of the business, you will miss out on many things with regards to your domestic market as well. For example, I usually recommend a set of dashboards and tools my clients can use when working with their overseas clients which are then often adopted for their domestic market.

Generally speaking, I find that having a detailed knowledge of their overseas competitors enables our clients to be better positioned in their domestic market. They usually develop a very acute understanding of their competitors which, in turn, helps them to remain competitive. They have seen these competitors in a number of different markets so they know what arguments to use to maintain their position. This is also a very good way to keep your domestic market and export businesses interconnected.

REAL-WORLD TOOL: Tips for Creating an Export-Focused Business

This guide sets out a few easy performance tasks which will help you engage your team on your exporting journey. It is really up to you to decide what is feasible and most adaptable to your business; this will also depend on your company culture and salary packages.

To download this tool, go the Downloads section of the Exportia website: www.exportia.com.au/downloads

12

Know the Language

At this point, I want to share with you my frustration when I meet people who do not understand the value and power of language. Having been brought up in Europe and with family living in different parts of Europe, I have always been immersed in language diversity. As a result, I have developed a passion for languages.

In the European market, businesspeople underestimate the amount of vital information they miss if they're not able to converse in the native language. In Europe, you will certainly find many people are able to speak English. The younger generation travel a lot and they make a point of learning English as an asset for their future careers. In contrast, when it comes down to the level of language qualifications of your target market, if you want your product to be installed by technicians in local garages, forget about using English when producing a training video.

The bottom line is that when you export to Europe, most of the time you will be competing with European companies. Be assured that your European competitor will have integrated multiple languages in their brochures, website, user manuals and marketing collateral. In most European countries, it is a legal obligation to have your user manual in the European language of the country you're selling to, particularly if you are selling to end-users.

I'm sure at this point that you're probably speculating about the advantages of Google Translate. My opinion on this tool is: if you are translating any marketing, sales, legal or technical documents that will be shared with clients, don't rely solely on Google Translate. Google Translate does not translate idiomatic expressions very well; most of the time it simply provides word-by-word translations. In the technological product industry, Google Translate does a poor job in terms of translating electrical or electronics information. Most importantly, the difference between a good and a bad translation involves whenever possible, ensuring the translator uses the same (or similar) terms that are used in your industry. And, sometimes the term used in the industry is the English one and not the German or French one! Only a human being with a brain can check for that (at least at present).

Remember, it is all about demonstrating to a French, Italian, German, Swedish or other European customer that it's easy to deal with your company. So, the first requirement is to talk to them in their own language. Sometimes, your distributors will also sell to several countries so they will appreciate having manuals available in several different languages.

My present benchmark in terms of a client who 'ticks all of the best practices boxes' for language diversity is a small company I am currently working with to develop their European footprint. They organised (without me suggesting it) to get their user manuals translated into twelve European languages. They built their website in French and German, plus commissioned my company to do the voice-over for their training videos in French and German. And guess what? Their French and German distributors *love* it! The easier you make it for your distributors to sell your product, the better it is for you. This is an ideal scenario because it removes any barriers from selling your product to your customers.

REAL-WORLD TOOL: Information Checklist – Rules for Using Google Translate

This information checklist is a very useful resource to help speed up the process involved in working with Australian clients who have received an enquiry in French or German. If our client is able to use Google Translate correctly to gain a broad understanding of the enquiry, it can save a lot of time for both of us.

To download this tool, go the Downloads section of the Exportia website: www.exportia.com.au/downloads

13

Price Reality Check

For companies without a lot of exporting experience, I sometimes find it useful to do a reality check on price levels before making any decisions to enter the European market. It is a very competitive market and, as I've mentioned previously, it has endured a number of tough economic periods. Consequently, European businesses have generally learnt to be extremely cost-effective through high automation, importing whenever possible, components from low-cost economies, and better processes. For this reason, you need to be able to gauge very early on if you're likely to be competitive price-wise or not.

For example, one of my clients had designed a product that was very technically clever and sophisticated. However, the associated costs were very high because of all the smart features in the product. As a result, I found it very hard to sell large volumes of this product because the European clients were used to much lower price levels. We still managed to sell a certain amount of the product and build the brand name profile; however, the next generation of the product will definitively take into account the required price point for the European market. It means we may offer a simpler product at an entry-level price and more advanced features at a premium price.

Establishing Realistic Prices for Products or Services

Now I know that you may already be thinking: 'How am I going to be able to check the price point for my product or service in the context of the European market?' There are several ways you can do this. The first things to consider are: Have you ever sold the product you want to export to the European market? What price did you sell it for? Did you have to heavily discount to get the deal signed? The answers to these questions will give you a good idea of the financial viability of exporting your product or service to Europe.

If you're aware that your European competitors sell products online through distributors who, in turn, directly sell to consumers, then you should be able to find their sales prices online. The only other way to find out this information is to interview test clients. By this, I mean potential end-users of your product or potential distributors. What you can do to ensure the process is cheap and fast is to pick a country at random where you believe you'd have the biggest potential and conduct your sample test there.

Another good way to check pricing levels is to actually buy a competitor's product in Europe from a European distributor. This is a quick and efficient method for you to determine price levels for various products and what value you get for them. I've done this for a few of my clients; it is a great way of obtaining market intelligence.

If you find these ideas too difficult to implement, you may prefer to buy a European competitor's product in your home country. However, it may not be as relevant because the

European competitor may have adjusted their price for your local market. If prices are higher in your home market than in other parts of the world, then it is quite likely that your European competitors have increased their prices for this market.

When undertaking this exercise, it is important to remember not to give up because you think your product is unique. Instead, try to find the closest equivalent product to yours. The objective is for you to gain a sense of what market price your future buyers have in mind. Are they used to cheap, simple products? Or are they already buying sophisticated products for a premium?

But what should you do if your product is a completely new form of 'disruptive' technology? For example, if you are generating electricity through a brand new process, try to get an idea of the cost of electricity production in Europe from different sources of energy (e.g. nuclear, hydro-electrical power plants, solar farms). This will assist you in seeing if your process stands a chance in the competitive European market.

What is the best approach if you think your prices may be too expensive for the European market? You may be aware that there are a lot of competitive products available in Europe with the same features as yours and with a much lower pricepoint. Does that mean you should stop right here and now? At this stage, you need to take a step back. If this is the case, as a business owner it is important for you to realise that competitors with cheaper products may enter your domestic market at any time so it is always useful to know about them. One of my Australian clients recently discovered that a European competitor had entered the Australian market with a very cheap low-quality solution. It just demonstrates that competition should be considered at global level.

Before launching into exporting to Europe, you need to quickly assess if your domestic market accepts a higher price point because it is a less competitive environment, and whether it is feasible for you to sell at a lower margin but to a larger European population used to buying cheaper (but equally sophisticated) products as yours. Alternatively, do you need to rethink and optimise your manufacturing process and supply chain in order to be able to export? These are a few considerations you need to review strategically at this stage. For example, a number of Australian small businesses have decided that the best option for them is to re-focus their attention to more high-end products. Consequently, they have shifted their focus to performing only high 'value-add' tasks in Australia – such as R&D – while the low-end part of their manufacturing is undertaken in Asia or in other parts of the world where labour costs are cheaper.

14

Product Range Focus

A key challenge some small or medium-sized businesses face is having a very broad range of products or solutions available on their catalogue. Consequently, they need to decide which products they're going to take to the European market before launching their exporting activities.

Marketing a large product range can be quite difficult as it requires more resources in order to develop the relevant user manuals and to promote a wide product range. Large multinationals are able to achieve this objective because they use their brand profile to promote themselves, and clients often base their purchasing decision on a brand name. When you are a small business and a newcomer to the European market, nobody knows your brand. As a result, you usually need to convince European customers to buy your product based on the associated 'value-add' which you have to be able to explain and position against your competitors.

Some examples to illustrate my point about the advantages of a narrow product range for a small business include:

- translating five user manuals rather than twenty into multiple languages is much faster and cheaper,
- focusing on one or two products in a magazine advertisement will have more impact than trying to communicate about many different products
- training your distributors' sales representatives is an easier task for a narrow range of products rather than training them on twenty products where they are then expected to remember each and every product 'value-add'.

In other words, try to make your life as easy as possible! Providing a clear focus for everyone engaged in your team is always the best option. And this focus can always be adjusted if you find that your product collection should be different (either narrower or broader) down the track. The situation will also change as your export sales grow.

Guidelines for Selecting your Initial Product Range for Export

At this stage, how do you select the initial product range for your business to export to Europe? First of all, while you were conducting your competitive analysis (see Section One), you would have observed which of your product(s) were likely to have the best sales outcomes in the European market. Likewise, you would have done a quick reality check on price so you would be aware which products should be competitive price-wise (see Chapter 13). These factors form the first selection criteria for determining which products you should be focusing your exporting efforts on.

The other selection criteria mentioned previously (see Chapter 6) is compliance with European specifications. You will have to select those products that are either certified for the European market or that have the best chances of achieving certification. To assess this, you should engage the services of a certification consultant to guide you through the process. Remember that product certification is a long and costly exercise so there are a lot of advantages in having a narrow range of products. For SME business owners, time and money are always important considerations in the exporting journey.

SECTION THREE

Begin Your European Enterprise on the Right Foot

15

Give it Your Best Shot

As an SME business owner considering exporting for the first time, it is vital that you give it your best shot. You need to be well prepared and to have done your homework.

Consider the following scenario: you have taken the first step in your exporting journey and have found a distributor to represent you in Europe. During the first months of this new collaboration, you have poor delivery service or there are faults with your product. As a result, it is highly likely that your distributor will not want to continue to work with you and may even completely drop you from their range. For this reason, it's important during these preliminary steps to ensure that your product and service are high quality in order to create a strong level of trust. As is often the case, people tend to remember more readily when something goes wrong. So, if your reputation is damaged in a particular export market, you will be viewed as 'the small American/Australian/Singaporean company which provides bad service'. Not only will your current distributor not want to work with you, but none of the other distributors in the marketplace will either because they won't want to gamble with the possibility of failure. Your company will be perceived as being a risk. Obviously, you can work hard to regain their trust, but it will take you a long time to build up a good reputation again. And, as small businesses, we are usually short of resources so we can't afford to squander time and money.

EXAMPLE CASE STUDY: Exporting to an Unfamiliar Industry Sector

To illustrate my point about the necessity of being well-prepared before launching into export markets, I will share with you an experience with one of my clients. This small business had just started to develop a new product range specifically with export markets in mind. The goal of the new range was to position the business within a more technical, high-quality, and specialised space and to differentiate the product from similar cheap products made in China. The business owner's objective was also to move into (and achieve higher sales volumes in) a completely new market vertical (i.e. the caravan and camping market as opposed to their traditional domestic vehicle market). His original business strategy had taken him around seven years to implement and to realise returns within the Australian market.

Working in the new European sector, it took us a long time to get initial sales for my client and we were not able to achieve a great deal of success overall. The reasons it took us so long to gain traction within Europe (even though there was the potential for good market opportunities) are quite complex. Our initial market study indicated that Europe has a huge caravan and camping market. Baby boomers are beginning to retire and their pensions enable them to spend quite substantially on leisure products. However, when we tried to market my client's new product range in Europe we encountered several challenges. My client didn't have a clear picture of the needs of the leisure industry segment as it was a completely new area to them – one that they weren't previously familiar with in their domestic market. Therefore, when it came to approaching the leisure industry market in Europe, we didn't have good customers stories and testimonials to tell potential clients. It took a while to establish sufficient trust for them to finally share with us the specifications they were looking for. These specifications were very different from the Australian domestic market so my client's product did not fully comply with the European customers' requirements. Consequently, we could only introduce the new product range to a limited number of target markets. Furthermore, my client's products were so innovative in comparison to what this market was traditionally used to that we needed to educate people while, at the same time, building the brand profile of the business.

Try to imagine doing all of this in a new market on the other side of the world where nobody is aware of your business. How long do you think it took us? In total, the process to build this exporting venture took us about five years. The important message here is that it is very challenging to start exporting to an industry segment in which you are not already completely familiar. Small businesses will always get faster results if they initially focus on the industry they know best and where they already have a proven track record. European clients are very interested to hear how things are done in their industry in other countries. You will always get more traction if you're able to talk directly to clients about their industry. This principle holds true for any commercial activity.

As a direct result of selling information technology solutions for IBM for a number of years, my exporting business, Exportia is usually able to quickly attract the attention of IT companies. Clients of mine have also told me they chose to work with my company because I have experience dealing with technical products and they felt confident that I'd have a good understanding of their technology. In addition, they liked the fact that I could relate to their industry. European clients are no different. They will relate to you more readily if you can share with them what you have done to solve problems in their industry within your own domestic market. In fact, it is quite likely that they may experience the same sort of problems!

Referring back to my case study example, while my client was aware it was strategic for his business to make the move into a new sector in the European market, he quickly understood it would take a long time for them to achieve results. With this background knowledge, he made the informed decision to persist with his original exporting goals and eventually received a good return further down the track.

Unfortunately, your business may not have sufficient financial resources to be able to wait for a return at a later stage. If this is the case, I strongly recommend that you concentrate on your strengths, which means focusing on the market segment where you have the most experience and customer testimonials. The European market may have slightly different needs from those of your domestic market, but it will just be a question of adapting to these new specifications. And adapting is much easier when you have a very good grasp of a specific industry.

16

Choose the Best Export Market

As discussed in previous chapters of this book, by now you should have assessed the export potential of the European market for your business. You would have researched and collected market statistics about the size of the market, as well as any initiatives that may be occurring within your industry from a European perspective. In addition, you may already have had a few enquiries from different European clients and you would have taken this opportunity to get to know them to better understand their needs.

From this information, you will have compiled your short-list of three or four countries and you will know which industry you are going to target within these countries. The goal now is for you to make a final decision about which country you are going to start exporting to. At this stage, my advice is to initially focus on only one country (or possibly two countries in the medium-term), especially if you have no prior export experience.

Scale Your Exporting Activities

From the outset, it's critical for small businesses to scale their approach to exporting. I know it can seem very glamorous to have London, Paris, or Milan at the bottom of your business card. The reality is that if you try to develop too many countries at the same time you will find it hard to get results from all of these different markets. The other challenge you will face is that the costs will be significant.

Whenever small businesses commence their exporting journey, I advise them to focus on one country only. Once they get this country right and generate sales from this market, they can then move to the next one. If you do have sufficient funds and can afford to chase several countries at a time, then good for you! However, what I usually find is that one or two countries will emerge as the best potential markets – often the largest European markets (e.g. Germany, France, UK, Spain, Italy). Small markets sometimes get started faster than larger markets (and generate initial sales until the small business owner's focus and budget is drawn in by the larger markets). Then the smaller markets become a bit neglected and stagnate for a while.

An example which demonstrates this point involves my client who had already engaged a number of distributors in several Scandinavian countries before commissioning my company to help them with their exporting operations. After a year spent working with this client, we started making some serious sales in the French market, found out the United Kingdom was not going to adopt their product, and that Germany would become a major market. At this stage, our priority was to give our full attention to France in order to ensure that consistent sales were generated in this market and we could take it from 'initial sales generation' to a more mature phase of 'consistent solid and growing sales'. For this to occur, we had to invest in more advertising in that particular market, as well as engaging agents to support the distributors. It was a significant investment for this company – a scenario that you should not attempt to undertake in too many countries at the same time or you will expose your business to too much risk.

So, my general advice is to focus on one country primarily and then you can research and prepare for others further down the track. The effect of going too fast too soon is that you might engage the wrong partners as a result of having an inadequate idea of that market. Then it becomes very difficult to reverse the relationship.

Criteria for Selecting an Export Country

One of the most common mistakes I've seen small businesses make when first deciding to export is to select a European country for the wrong reasons – whether it's for family reasons, familiarity with the language or because the business owner's children are currently studying in one of these countries. I have even seen people make a decision based on the fact that they find Italy or France attractive holiday destinations. I know it sounds hard to believe but this is the reality. I have worked with many Australian companies and some of them systematically target the UK market because they share a common language. This is a fair call as it does make things easier if there is no language barrier; I do recognise this point. However, it can only work well if you have already validated that the United Kingdom has potential for your product or service.

What is the problem with choosing the wrong country for your exporting operation? On average, it takes me between three months to two years to begin to achieve results in an export market. Consequently, if you imagine that you had spent two years exporting to a market where your product has little potential, this would mean very slow results and low export sales. Exporting requires an investment of money and time and, generally speaking, small businesses are short of both. So, the objective is to select the country where you will have the biggest chances of success.

Identifying the Right Country for Exporting

Although statistics are very useful in helping you form a broad picture of the market, you need to develop a thorough understanding about which European country is ready to buy your product straight away.

The process I usually follow for my clients is to interview two types of main players (both end-users as well as potential distributors) in three to five different European countries. In some industries, such as in the medical sector, I try to interview influencers such as doctors who are opinion leaders in their particular discipline. This is not a hard-sell type of approach – it is purely a fact-finding exercise at this stage. Essentially, the aim is to gather feedback about what you have to offer. At the end of this chapter, I have included a link where you can download a list of examples of the type of questions you could ask in order to gain as much insight as possible.

What I do to prepare the interviews that I or my team will conduct on behalf of our clients is to find out from them what selection criteria they use to decide which countries are best suited to their business. I ask them to determine what the optimum conditions are to sell their product in an ideal world. Some examples to illustrate this point include: clients in the medical sector looking for countries where there is a specific reimbursement scheme for medical devices used to cure a specific pathology, and clean technology companies seeking to understand which European country is the most advanced in terms of adopting clean energy. In this case, they are likely to be interested in a country where the government has established a scheme to subsidise the installation of insulation in houses.

When you interview the main industry players, ensure that you maximise the opportunity by asking leading questions that will provide you with relevant information about your selection criteria. Internet research to gather statistics is great; however, nothing beats talking to people in your industry about their everyday working lives. All the preliminary research you will have already done will help you to be more focused in your questioning.

The trick here is to eliminate any pressure from the situation and from the person you're interviewing. At this stage, you are not selling to them; you are interviewing them because they are experts in their country within a specific industry. I recommend that you actually tell them: 'I chose you because you are *the* largest distributor in your sector' or because 'You are *the* most published doctor on this pathology'. You will be amazed to discover how much information people are willing to share with you if you are really honest and clearly explain what you are seeking.

REAL-WORLD TOOL: Research Resource – Country Selection Mind Map

I developed this mind mapping resource to help you to create a short-list of three to four European countries which are the best options for exporting for your business. You can modify this tool so that it fits your own selection criteria. Each industry is different and you will need to fine-tune this mind map according to your needs.

To download this tool, go the Downloads section of the Exportia website: www.exportia.com.au/downloads

17

Select the Appropriate Industry

While working with numerous SMEs during the past decade, I have observed one common mistake made by business owners that I want to share with you – and this mistake is most prevalent within the start-up world. Typically, small businesses set out to target too many industries at one time. In an export scenario, it can be very difficult to manage and can be also quite costly and yield very slow results. For example, let's take the example of a small business in the IT industry which creates software used in the construction industry, government and real estate. Within their domestic market, the IT business caters for the needs of these three industries and is well established in all of them. Ideally, they would like to be able to replicate this successful strategy in an export market. However, for a small business to approach three different industries at the same time involves preparing three different pitches, as well as three different sets of customer testimonials. Very often it also requires engaging three different distributors, with each distributor having their own particular specialisation. What this basically means is that your resources and attention are spread over three different areas. Consequently, it will take you three times longer to prepare all of your marketing material and three times longer to attract potential clients' attention in the three different industries.

What if, instead, you decided to commence your exporting operation one industry at a time? Let's say you pick one industry where you have previously had good results: for the sake of this exercise, we'll choose the construction industry. Now you just have to get one testimonial from one of your satisfied clients in the construction industry and also find one partner who is active in this industry. You then have more time available to lobby the European construction industry and work on finding influencers within it. Your team is under less pressure because they have one specific task to do instead of three. Furthermore, you can advertise in one magazine instead of three.

If you initially focus all of your exporting efforts in one specific industry, you will get good results faster. And, as a result, you will become well-known within that industry much more quickly. For small businesses, long-term success is all about focusing your time, energy and resources in the right place in order to maintain balance. It is very important to maintain that balance in export markets, because exporting is an inherently risky and cost-intensive activity for a small business.

18

Interviewing Market Prospects in Europe

Now that you have a better idea about which country and which industry to focus on, I'll give you some tips regarding how I approach the information gathering process. I do a lot of interviewing of European market prospects on my clients' behalf. If there's a degree of confidentiality involved and my client is not ready to disclose that they are planning to move into the European market, I usually introduce myself as Exportia and say that we are currently conducting a market research project and, as part of this project, we would like to understand XYZ. I will then describe in detail the market information that we want to find out more about. If our client is happy for us to disclose their company name, I usually explain that our client – company XYZ – is contemplating entering the European market in the immediate future and that we are trying to assess which country has the best potential for their product. For this reason, we are interested in hearing their feedback. For example: What do they think about this product? Do they see a need for it? Letting the overseas clients know that we are in the preliminary stages and are just conducting market research removes any feeling of pressure for them. We don't want to sell anything to them right now; we are simply seeking their expert advice. This approach works very well. At this stage, you can then ask them: 'If we were to select your country for our exporting activities, I may need to contact you again – would that be okay with you?' And guess what? Nine times out of ten the response is 'Yes!' If this market turns out to be a profitable option for you down the track, you already have an entry point which saves you a lot of time at later stages.

Identifying and Approaching the Best Prospects

Now you may be wondering: 'How can I identify these European people if I am not based over there? What if they don't speak English?' Of course, the best and fastest approach is to get assistance from a specialist consultant or agency such as ours. This is because we can readily obtain all of this information through our network via phone interviews in several European languages. We don't have to travel to many different places to obtain it.

If you don't have access to an exporting specialist, there are several ways you can approach this task yourself. One of the best sources of information about the European market is industry trade shows. Generally speaking, one trade show per industry with European or international coverage is usually held every year or every two years. Trade shows are a good way to identify key people within your industry; however, you may find it hard to interview them on the spot at these events because they are there specifically for their clients. Try to do whatever is possible and, at the very minimum, seek out the key person and their contact details so that you're able to interview them at a later stage. It's very easy to waste time during trade shows so I would advise you to prepare three to six months in advance. Don't overlook the European holidays – it's much harder to reach people from 15 July to 15 August, and Christmas holidays are also a down time (20 December to 5 January). The best approach is to have organised a number of meetings beforehand, since business people are extremely busy at these trade shows. You need to understand which days are designated for industry professionals and which are for the general public. Ensure that you attend on the professional days. Ideally, arrange meetings well in advance or at least find out which time of the day is easier for them to spend ten minutes having a conversation with you. Be on the ball and have your five quick questions ready.

Another way to set up an interview with an industry expert is to check out speakers at congresses and conferences. Usually they will have online versions of their presentation and it's quite likely they will have published a number of research papers. If they are an opinion leader in their field, these experts will usually have a very clear vision regarding what is happening at the European level. Moreover, they are often able to tell you about differences between practices in different countries. In my company, we often use this technique to acquire information for our clients. For example, at one time we were looking for information for a client project about a medical device for sterilisation of hospital equipment. We interviewed the president in charge of an association responsible for sharing best-practice for sterilisation among French hospitals. We'd identified her because she was systematically presenting at European congresses. She had an in-depth knowledge of the different sterilisation practices in various European countries. In this way, we were able to easily shortlist the top two countries where this medical device would be readily accepted and compatible with local practices.

LinkedIn is a great online social media tool for identifying key industry professionals by their company positions. You can then target them or ask their advice about who is the best contact person within their industry. Once you have identified these key people, it is important to stick to your goals when interviewing them. You need to find out what the problem is or what incentive these European clients have to buy your product now. This is what is going to guide you in selecting the best European options for your business.

Ask them direct questions such as:

- Do you see a need for our product in your market?
- Would you buy this product?
- If not, why?

From the outset, it is vital that you select the European country with the most urgent need for your product.

19

Decide on the Right Export Channels

A common mistake for many small business owners when they initially decide to launch into exporting is to engage the first European distributor who approaches them. Often, the small business is very excited to have been contacted by an overseas company and engages them without conducting any due diligence. They simply think that by engaging a distributor they will generate extra cash, which is a bonus as they had not even considered exporting. Then, down the track when they do become serious about exporting, they discover that this distributor is not a good fit for their particular business.

Define Your Ideal Distributor Profile

One of the tasks I consistently advise my clients to do during the early stages of their exporting journey is to properly define their partner or distributor profile. The general recommendation within the exporting industry is to partner with distributors so that their sales representatives will then sell your products.

By partnering with distributors, you are able to tap into their geographical client base.

In my opinion, there are only a few exceptions to this general principle: for example, you have a large company that has sufficient resources to establish a subsidiary in Europe, with all the legal support necessary to manage risk along the way. However, I imagine that if you are currently reading this book, you do not fall into this category. The other exception is if you are operating in a very niche market and have only a few major clients in each country. In this case, it does not always make sense to have a distributor look after them and you may be better off partnering with another type of company (e.g. sales agent).

Before engaging with distributors or partners, you need to define the ideal distributor profile for your business. The best place to start is by reflecting on the profile of distributors you have already worked with. Next, try to identify the type of companies they are and what they do that worked well for you in terms of selling your product. You may not be able to locate this exact type of distributor in every single European country, but you do need to be able to leverage your experience.

To select an appropriate distributor for your business, you need to be very clear about which industry you are targeting and the type of clients associated with that particular industry. For example, if my target market is the public sector, I would most likely be targeting local councils of cities with ten to fifty million people. In this scenario, my target customer is the person managing all of the assets owned by the city (e.g. gardening equipment, vehicles fleets). Once you are very clear about your customer profile, you will be in a good position to find distributors with this type of specific clientele in their portfolio and who are already selling other types of products that are complementary to yours. You need to ask the question: 'What type of similar products are my typical distributors selling in addition to my product?' These complementary products may also be competitors' products. The other important consideration is what role you want the distributor to play for you. You should determine what tasks you want them to do for you in the market besides sales. This might include such criteria as after-sales service or repairs, and training.

Possibly one of the most important factors that will help you succeed in your exporting journey is your distributor's profile. You need to determine what benchmarks will work best for you to ensure that you are able to maximise your sales. For a small business in the high-tech sector, some example questions that will guide you to head in the right direction include:

- Are they a large company or a small business?
- How broad is their product range?
- Do they sell high-end technical products?
- Are they mainly selling to customers via a catalogue?
- How large is their salesforce?
- Are they a wholesaler? Do they sell to a network of resellers or directly to end-users?
- What profile do their sales reps have? Do they spend more time on the road or are they in the office preparing marketing campaigns? Are they technically orientated? What are their sales incentives?
- Are they regional or nationally based?

To give you an example from my own exporting business, at one time I realised that the sales representative I was trying to encourage to sell more of one of my client's products had no salary incentives linked to sales. I was surprised to find out that he was not paid on commission. It would have been helpful to have known this information in the first place.

Recognise the Differences between Export and

Domestic Markets

A few years ago, I made the difficult decision to cease working with a particular client. We had begun exploring opportunities for them in a European country – visiting end-users to get a feel for the market and generating initial leads, as well as connecting with potential partners. My challenge in dealing with this client stemmed from the fact that he wanted to do business in Europe exactly the same way as in his home market in Australia. In Australia, he sold his business solution directly to end-users. This involved him undertaking the majority of the sales and he also employed a sales representative. In Europe, he did not want to have to deal with any middle man since he preferred to sell directly to end-users. After conducting a couple of fact-finding trips to Europe with him, I made several recommendations in order to take the export project a step further. I was very aware that, given the fact that we were targeting end-users in the public sector, there was no way we would win any tenders if we responded simply as a small Australian company. In this instance, the best tactic was to partner with a European company with prior experience responding to government tenders and which was very familiar with both the process and the buyers in that sector. Unfortunately, I was not able to get my point across to my client; he insisted that we should keep visiting these end-users regardless. I knew his approach would take us nowhere and, subsequently, he would not get a good outcome with his exporting activities. For this reason, I decided to terminate our working relationship, citing the reasons for my decision (how dare I!).

The lesson from this story is that small businesses need to partner with companies that are well established in the export market they want to enter if they're to have any chance of success. You may currently be selling directly to end-users in your domestic market; however, in export markets, doing direct sales involves creating a company, hiring people locally and being well informed about local laws – just to name a few factors for consideration. I do not recommend this approach for most small businesses as it is too risky financially. You may ultimately want to work towards this type of business structure in Europe; however, don't begin this way. The best option is usually to work with partners (or distributors) to leverage their expertise and knowledge of the local market.

REAL-WORLD TOOL: Checklist – Profile of Your Ideal European Distributor

This checklist is designed to help you to develop your ideal European distributor profile. You can refine this profile as you progress on your export journey and you learn more about the distributors that work best for you.

To download this tool, go the Downloads section of the Exportia website: www.exportia.com.au/downloads

20

Safeguard Your Business Interests

By this stage of your exporting journey you will have carefully considered which country and which industry are the best fit for your business export activities. Likewise, you will have reviewed your product range and selected the products you are going to focus on within your export market. The next steps involve you finding out how to protect your intellectual property related to these products, as well as establishing appropriate pricing levels.

Protect Your Intellectual Property

As I mentioned in Chapter Six, when it comes to protecting your intellectual property, an IP lawyer is your best friend. Most innovative companies are well-versed in the patent registration process and would have already protected their innovation through a patent quite early in the process prior to their product reaching the commercialisation stage. At this point, I strongly recommend that you review your current position in terms of relevant patents and trademarks in all of the countries in which you are intending to commercialise your product. It's important to undertake this process in those countries where your product has most potential – or preferably in the entire European Union if you can afford it.

Appropriate Pricing Levels for Export Markets

When you first engage the services of a European distributor, you will need to validate their interest and then share pricing information. It is important that you don't share your price lists with distributors straight away. For example, if you are a small high-tech company, the success of your business is not solely dependent upon pricing. It's also about your innovative solutions and the difference your product can make for an industry or for a typical client problem. Only share your price lists with distributors you consider to be the most likely prospects to work with and when the possibility of working together seems promising. You don't want your price list to be in the hands of those distributors you won't be conducting business with. Nevertheless, at this stage, it is a good idea to prepare your initial price list – even if it's likely to require adjustment down the track.

In my business, I see a lot of the same mistakes occurring as a result of companies' ignorance about pricing levels, so it is important to thoroughly research this area and be well prepared. A few simple rules about pricing in export markets are outlined for you below:

Ex-Works

The easiest approach when you are first starting out with a distributor's price list is to simply use an ex-works (EXW) price list. This involves listing your prices in Euros ex-factory; at this stage you do not need to include freight costs and import duties. Keep it simple at first. Further down the track you can use other

Incoterms (i.e. international rules for the interpretation of trade terms) to make your distributor's life easier. Always mention the city and country after each Incoterm. For example, you may be providing products which are ex-works Sydney Australia. Ensure that you always use the latest Incoterms.

Euros

I recommend you prepare price lists for distributors in Euros for as many European countries as possible. To maintain consistency, avoid having a distributor's price listed in numerous currencies, such as Swedish Krones or Swiss Francs. Managing multiple currencies can be difficult so get your distributors to do the maths for you. In the few countries that have not adopted the Euro as their currency, it is still often the case that they will accept Euros. The only caveat to that is the United Kingdom where businesses still like to deal in British Pounds.

Validity

To avoid any possible problems, give your price list a validity to protect your business from significant exchange range variation. At the same time, your distributors will find it challenging if you are constantly changing your prices. They operate by referring to catalogues that have a fixed price. For this reason, they can't afford to change prices continually because these catalogues are usually issued for a full year. So, if you can provide at least six months validity, it will be a good option for your business. If you can commit to twelve months, it will be even better (and simpler) for you and your distributors to manage.

Freight Costs

Request a few quotes from freight forwarders for a typical minimum order of your products in order to get an idea of what freight costs you will need to charge your distributors.

Construct several scenarios for air freight and sea freight so that you are aware of what the possible volume breaks are. In this way, you'll be able to determine which products (along with associated quantities) are more profitable to ship by sea rather than air. Depending on the size of your product, it is important for you to develop a good understanding of this issue.

HS Code

At this stage, you will also need to be aware of the Harmonized Commodity Description and Coding System – also referred to as the Harmonized System or simply HS – developed by the World Customs Organization (WCO). This is an international identification number that enables customs in Europe (in whichever country) to assess which import tariff they are going to charge your distributor. It is important for you to know how much custom duties the distributor is going to pay when importing your product, so you will be required to provide them with these codes.

To find out what these international identification codes are you will need to provide a description of each product to a customs agency in a European market or to a domestic freight forwarder that is used to dealing with Europe. You can also research this information yourself by checking out the European Union website.

Recommended Retail Price or End-User Prices

When you first commence exporting, you need to consider the recommended retail price for your products. What will be your recommended retail price or your recommended end-user price in Euros?

The first place to start is to refer to your domestic market's recommended retail price (excluding GST). In addition, while you are assessing your European competition, browse online to check out their recommended retail prices. Depending on your price positioning versus competitive product, you can then set your price levels accordingly.

It is important to be aware that not all European countries have the same value-added tax rates (VAT) so at this stage exclude VAT from your recommended end-user price list to help keep things simple. Of course, if you are selling to consumers, you will need to check the VAT in that particular country before setting your recommended retail price.

Be Aware of Your Distributor's Margin

You will need to find the right balance between, on the one hand, your costs and the profit margin you need to make and, on the other hand, your recommended retail price in Europe. For that, you also need to know the margin that your distributor requires. In some cases, distributors sell to retailers. Next, you will also need to make sure they can have a margin that they're happy with. You need to check how it all balances out and how everyone can make sufficient margin to be motivated to sell your products.

REAL-WORLD TOOL: Price List Template

I have developed this Price List Template for my clients to help them start the discussion with a distributor. In this resource, the Incoterm used is ex-works, but can be changed to another Incoterm.

To download this tool, go the Downloads section of the Exportia website: www.exportia.com.au/downloads

21

Exporting Market Groundwork

Before deciding to engage with distributors or potential export clients, it's a good idea to prepare a company profile and value proposition to assist you with marketing your business.

Prepare Your Company Profile

Your company profile can be the one you use for your home country. It should include the date you started your business, the size of your company, and provide details about the ownership (especially if it is a family company). Don't incorporate an image of the flag of your home country or any reference to 'proudly' before the phrase 'made in' to avoid any misinterpretation by Europeans. European people can be quite sensitive when it comes to the use of flags and other nationalistic symbols as they are often used by right-wing racist groups.

When it comes to describing your value proposition, try to make it as compelling as possible to the specific European industry you're targeting. Earlier in this book, I advised you to analyse your competition, so you should now be aware of how to position your product and its benefits to a specific industry. Likewise, incorporating a few testimonials from European customers or from your home country is a great addition to your company profile.

Ideally, this information should be available as a brochure in PDF format that can be printed for trade shows or for client meetings. It is important to remember that your brochure needs to be brief so it can translated into multiple European languages in a cost-efficient manner.

Customer Case Studies and Testimonials

Case studies and customer testimonials are very powerful marketing tools to use when exporting into the European market. Ideally, if you already have a European client you can approach them to ask if they would be willing to become a case study. If not, simply provide a case study from your domestic market. Make it very brief; simply get your client to explain the problem they experienced and why they decided to switch to your product. Most importantly, it is valuable to show what they gained (or saved) as a result of using your solution. Ensure the case study is industry-specific, keep the text to a minimum and include a few photos. Photos are a very powerful method of communicating information, so choose one or two photos that show a scenario in which your product is being used. Once again, you need to be prepared to translate your case studies into multiple European languages, so keep them brief.

As you gradually acquire more export clients in European markets, you can start to develop a library of case studies. If you have sufficient budget, I also recommend that you create film testimonials and incorporate them on your website and on YouTube. For example, it is really effective to film your product in the environment in which it is used. In my experience working within my business, Exportia, I have discovered that clients love to hear how the same type of companies as theirs conduct business in other countries.

Another valuable technique is to take your clients on field visits to other clients' sites. In situations where there is no direct competition between the two organisations, it can be the best form of advertising for your company and your product to take prospective clients to visit one of your existing clients' sites in another European country. For example, if you are selling high-tech products, it can represent a significant risk for your prospective clients to switch to a new solution. It is very powerful for your prospective clients to visit other organisations that have already implemented your solution and can testify that they have received all the support they needed from you.

Of course, while the ideal scenario is a visit to a site, this can often be tricky or impractical to organise. At the very minimum, you can organise a conference call with your current client and your prospective client. Sometimes it may be that your prospective client doesn't want you – the supplier – to be involved. This is fair enough; don't push to be present at the conference call. Instead, simply schedule the call but don't participate. You may need to organise the services of an interpreter to facilitate the communication exchange.

SECTION FOUR

All Systems Go!

22

Make Export Markets Your Priority

When I'm working with a small business client to develop their export markets, the thing that frustrates me the most is the fact that, in some cases, their domestic market takes priority over my efforts to secure international business for them. I do understand that the domestic market is what provides the 'bread and butter' for small businesses as well as funding for exporting activities. However, if the export progress is constantly delayed, there will never be any opportunity for success.

What frequently happens is that the European clients are the ones that are served last. However, they are the clients that you absolutely need to get on board. They must be able to see that your business is responsive, even though you are operating from overseas. For export clients, your response time and customer service have to be excellent. This is a common error because the export market is not yet generating sales so the company's sales and marketing teams tend to allocate it a lower priority. It then becomes very challenging for the person in charge of exporting operations to do a good job developing these export markets.

European clients need to feel you are focused on them and that they are important to you. Otherwise, any export activities you do undertake are counter-productive.

At the opposite end of the spectrum, some of my clients have geared their business so they have a strong focus on European sales and consequently they obtain amazing results with us.

What to Consider when Selecting a Distributor

A common scenario I often observe amongst my clients is that of a small business being approached online by an overseas distributor and delighted to potentially start exporting, the small business signs up the distributor immediately. It is a very common mistake, so my advice to you is to *be picky*! Don't be scared to be selective even though you are a small business. It may sound simplistic, but make sure you evaluate potential distributors thoroughly before signing them up. Sometimes small businesses are so excited to be contacted by a European distributor that they even forget to assess them properly before starting to negotiate with them.

You will actually be considered by overseas buyers as being very professional if you explain to potential distributors that you're evaluating several alternatives in the market before making a final decision. They will come to the conclusion that you know what you are doing. Moreover, it creates competitive tension in the market, which means that, as a small business owner, you're in a better bargaining position when dealing with distributors.

Assessing Potential Distributors

In Chapter 19, I advised you to create a preliminary profile for your ideal European distributor. It is important that you now assess your potential distributor against this profile. When you contact them, appraise them and ask questions to gain more market intelligence. There are a few things that you will only be able to discover as a result of interviewing them. For example, I know that my high-tech clients require a European distributor who is going to make the effort to demonstrate their product, set up trials, collect feedback and push the sale for them.

It is also critical that the distributor is willing to share plenty of feedback from the field with you. A common trait of successful businesses is that they continually develop products based on their customers' feedback and they use this feedback to prioritise projects based on volume forecasts. So, it's important that the distributor you do end up engaging is able to provide you with this feedback, In other words, it needs to be embedded in their company culture – a criteria you can only properly gauge by interviewing them.

Your future distributor will need to initially target the clients you are seeking, so their sales and marketing mindset should be aligned with yours. Be very clear as to which segment you have had the most success with in your local market. For example, should your distributor target a network of dealers or sell to large companies or to SMEs? After deciding that, you need to define what type of after-sales support they are able to provide you with. Is it just level one support or can they offer you more? What processes will be established for this level of support? Ask them if they will charge you for this service and, if so, how will the payment system work.

The other important criteria to establish is what marketing tools the distributor is going to use to promote your products. Does this approach fit with your company's current marketing strategy or ideas? You need to ask them for examples of their sales reach and the type of marketing campaigns they usually undertake. For example, do they attend trade fairs? Do they have an aggressive online presence? In which magazines do they advertise? How large are their databases of business contacts?

Another major item for you to evaluate when selecting a distributor is to check if your pricing levels are going to work in terms of their mark-up structure. What margins do they usually request for themselves? How many layers of mark-up will there be (i.e. wholesaler/dealer/consumer or distributor consumer)? How much mark-up does each 'layer' expect? Next, check where this pricing structure sits in relation to your recommended retail price (RRP).

If you are working with a large retailer/distributor, ask them for their suppliers' conditions and clarify whether or not any financial contribution will be asked for further down the track (e.g. end-of-year discount, contribution to a catalogue). It is important for you to take this information into account in your overall pricing. You also need to be aware of the profile of the distributor's sales representatives. What is their educational and career background? Are they technically educated or is their training more marketing-focused? Don't hesitate to ask them how they are paid – is it based on sales, on margins, or on profit?

A further very crucial point to consider is the range of products your distributor offers. You need to make the decision between being listed as one product amongst a limited number of other products, and being included in a large catalogue with an extensive range of different products. It comes down to making a decision based on the size of the distributor: is a small distributor the best option for you or would a large national distributor suit you better? It's critical to think about this issue in-depth because, in terms of speed to market, each option will have a very different outcome. For example, you may require a solution that provides a quick entry into the market with a small distributor if you need to achieve rapid export sales.

As you are now aware, there is a long list of questions that I suggest you ask potential distributors to determine the best fit for your business. You can also check to find out if you need to incorporate any additional questions. The majority of these points will be applicable to most SMEs. Carefully evaluating your potential future distributors will definitely increase your chances of success in export markets. For a small business, the cost of engaging the wrong distributor can be very high. Most SMEs can't afford to have no return on investment. When I choose a distributor for a client, I understand that this decision is critical because my client needs to have a return on investment from our services. And it would be costly for both of us if their business goes down the wrong track.

One or Many Distributors – Which is Best?

At this stage, you may be wondering how many distributors you should consider engaging to assist you with your business' exporting operations. This question has several consequences for your business. In the first instance, the answer really depends on the type of distributors you ultimately require for your particular business. For example, within your market, there will probably be only one or two major national distributors.

Next, you will need to consider how many people you can readily train. For example, one of my clients decided to only engage one major national distributor because this company had 200 sales representatives. For a small business, it would take a lot of time to train and support all of these sales reps. Clearly for this organisation the most suitable option was to have just one national distributor. You need to be able to provide an excellent service to the distributors you do end up selecting. There is no point in having too many of them and not being able to support them.

23

Identifying and Contacting Potential Distributors

Having conducted preliminary research to find out background information about distributors relevant to your particular export market segment, it is now time to identify and approach potential distributors in order to engage their services for your business.

Identifying the Right Distributors for Your Business

Having now defined your ideal distributor profile, how can you identify who are the right distributors for your business? Of course, a Google keyword search is always a good place to start. However, there are some other very simple methods to identify those distributors or partners who best match your ideal distributor profile. For example, you can conduct an online search of your competitors' products and find out who is selling them. You can also check the 'Where to Buy' sections on your competitors' websites.

At this point, you should also be aware of the type of complementary products usually sold in conjunction with your products. For example, if your business manufactures lawn mowers and the distributors who usually sell your product also sell small tools of a certain brand for removing weeds, you need to search online to find out who sells that brand. You will be able to do this by researching the 'Where to Buy' section of their website and then checking out their distributors' list. Another easy way to find this information is to check the exhibitors list in the trade show catalogues for your industry in that particular country. All of the major distributors should be listed in it. In addition, you can get in touch with your relevant industry association and check out their list of members. Likewise, you can interview an opinion leader or an industry influencer to find out some additional names. This is often a very good way to discover the most useful information. You can quiz them and ask what they think about those distributors you have already identified online as possible options for your business.

There are several relevant databases available for purchase in the marketplace, but they are often a bit clunky to use and their subscription fee can be prohibitive, so I don't often refer to them. However, when it comes to conducting due diligence, they can be very helpful for checking financial data to determine the financial health of an organisation. Each country will usually have its own financial records providers.

Wherever possible, I like to tap into my business network to find out pertinent names. Think about the people in your network and ask them for their advice. You might also like to consider asking end-users where they buy their supplies. If you know an end-user, ask them which distributors they currently deal with. If they don't use a distributor themselves, ask them who they know who could share this information with you.

Once you have identified your list of potential distributors (ideally from five to ten as a minimum), you need to classify and rate them against your ideal distributor profile. Be open to suggestions and be aware that, in a particular country, there might be distributors with different profiles from what you'd initially expected. This is fine – you just need to evaluate them and integrate them into your overall selection criteria.

Approaching Your Preferred Distributors

When doing business in Europe, you will definitely save time if you're able to talk to people in their own language. Your positioning and message need to be very clear; by now you will have done your homework on your European competitors so you are able to readily demonstrate how your products and/or services differ from those of your competitors and what value you can offer end-users.

Depending on the size of the distributor, I recommend you start by targeting the purchasing manager, the product manager, or the head of the technical department in charge of your product line. For very technical products (like most of the products I deal with in my business), I don't usually target the purchasing manager because he or she is rarely technically savvy and won't automatically recognise the benefits of a new product over what they currently have. Rather, they tend to push back – making such claims as, 'We have no need for that type of approach'. So you need to ensure that you do some research before involving the purchasing department in the loop. This might involve seeking out those organisations for whom the following statements are an issue: 'We currently have a lot of product returns due to faults'; 'The products we currently stock do not meet our requirement in terms of power'; or 'That product line is bit old-fashioned and we need to find new innovative products'. In this way, you'll be in a better position to contact the director of the business or the purchasing manager and explain why they should include your product in their range.

Another way of approaching potential distributors is to do so when you visit or exhibit at your industry trade show. When it comes to actually contacting distributors, the only methods that I have personally found to be effective are getting on the phone, visiting their stand at a trade show, or asking for an introduction from someone in my network. Depending on the country, I find that using social media professional networks such as LinkedIn can also be helpful.

As mentioned earlier, I recommend that you don't share your price list straight away with anyone; validate their interest first. Only share pricing information with those distributors who you perceive as being keen and engaged. You don't want your pricing to be everywhere in the market. However, it is fine to share your recommended retail prices early on as they provide a good starting point for discussion.

It is important to find out each distributors' decision cycle prior to engaging them. When distributors print their product catalogues, they have very specific decision timelines and you need to be aware of these dates to ensure that you don't miss an opportunity. In Europe, trade shows are very important events for conducting business, so knowing the date of the major trade show in that specific country (and in Europe in general) is critical.

As an example of a decision cycle of a specific distributor: the critical timelines for one of my clients who has their product range distributed in a specific European country is as follows:

- By end of May – product selection
- By end of July – provision of text and images for catalogue, plus European Union norms compliance certificates; prices are negotiated.

- By end of August – catalogues are printed
- End of August – largest European trade show
- End of September – largest national trade show.

If you enter the decision cycle at the wrong time, you will have to wait for a whole year before they are again in a position to consider your product. Occasionally, distributors will also offer a new product release during the year. This can be a good test run for your products, so try to find out if (and when) it is available.

REAL-WORLD TOOL: Interview Guide – Identify and Engage Your Ideal Distributor

I developed this interview guide for you to use to determine the interest of potential distributors prior to appointing them. The objective of this tool is to step you through the distributor evaluation process, but also to explain how to close the interview; the follow-up actions are as important as the meeting itself. As a result of this interview, you will have an idea of the distributors' motivation (depending of course, on how responsive they were during your meeting).

To download this tool, go the Downloads section of the Exportia website: www.exportia.com.au/downloads

24

Negotiating Trading Terms

Negotiating trading terms with your distributors is always a tricky process. However, it is something that you should not be scared of as a small business owner. My advice is to start with the terms that are good for your business. Developing a good understanding of the Incoterms mechanism is essential. There are some simple exporting training programs available that take you through this process and it is very important that you get your team up to speed on this. In the case of Australian businesses, the Australian Institute of Export offers good training workshops. The people in your organisation who are responsible for invoicing and liaising with freight companies will need to have a good understanding of the various systems so they're able to use the right terms on the invoice. The trading terms also need to be clear to facilitate shipping and ensure that transportation is problem-free.

With reference to trading terms, I will share with you a real-life example of one of my clients. I had been in touch with the chairman of this particular company a few times, so he knew what services we offered our clients and was well aware that France was one of our countries of expertise. One day, I received a call from him requesting my help with the French market and asking my opinion about two distributors. The distributors seemed to be fine; however, after chatting to the CEO I realised that the trading terms that had been negotiated by the European representative were very problematic. The rep had negotiated terms which included free shipping, 'because that is what you do in Europe'. However, when you are a small business shipping products by air from Australia to Europe you can't afford not to charge for freight costs. The other problem was that sometimes the Australian manufacturer also paid VAT and did not receive a credit for it (there are procedures in place for recovering VAT). When I started checking the price lists sent to the distributors, I observed that the terms were a bit vague. So, I recommended that the CEO keep the same price list and state that the trading terms were ex-works, which means that the manufacturer provides the goods at the factory and the buyer arranges for the goods to be collected. In this way, the buyer pays for the shipping, import tax and local VAT. When I explained this to him he said, 'Do you really think we can do that? I was told that Europeans would never want to deal in this manner. Our French distributor is so large I was always told they would never accept that arrangement.' My response was, 'Yes, we can!' So together we formatted the initial price list, clearly stating that the prices were ex-works from Australia and providing the relevant city location. Next, after carefully considering the process, we established the new terms with the distributor. I then contacted the other distributors one by one to introduce myself and explain the new arrangement. At this point, it was quickly decided that these terms would be implemented with every European distributor.

Further down the track, a few distributors requested that our client organise the freight and that they be charged for it. Consequently, the French distributor simply had to pay import duties and VAT. A year later, we implemented a price list which included freight costs to each regional logistic platform. In this case, the Incoterm (an internationally recognised system which clearly states the different responsibilities of the buyer and the seller) we used was Delivery at Place (DAP). The good thing about DAP is that the distributor is still responsible for clearing the import duties and paying for VAT. This whole process was such a relief for my client, particularly when they were able to see how easy it was to implement. Any fear they'd previously felt regarding losing a major distributor quickly vanished. At the end of the day, if a distributor is really interested in your product, they won't give up. And if they are really not happy about the trading terms, they will tell you and start negotiating with you.

So, my recommendation to you is to implement trading terms that you consider to be acceptable for your business However, in terms of currency, it really makes the life of your distributors much easier if you're able to produce your price list in Euros. You will need to manage the exchange rate fluctuation or, alternatively, open a bank account that deals in Euros. Contact your bank to discuss the various options.

Setting Your Pricing Levels

When dealing with distributors, another aspect to consider is to set your pricing levels in accordance with volume breaks. I strongly recommend that you provide volume breaks to your customers. People like to have the feeling they are getting a good deal. For example, you can offer customers the terms whereby, if they order twenty items, they pay the unit price, if they order fifty items there is a better unit price,and if they order 100 items they get an even better price. Finally, if they bulk order 500 items you will provide them free shipping.

One of my clients adopts another strategy in his business. He says to his customers, 'Here is my best price. That's it!' As far as he is concerned, he gives them the best possible conditions so there is no reason for them to complain. My response to him is: 'When the distributors start to increase their volume of sales, they are going to come back to you with a request to improve your original price. This is just the way things work.' Moreover, it is valuable for your business to give your customers the incentive to order larger quantities. They may only need to order thirty-five units; however, if they see that by ordering fifty units they will get a much better deal, they are more likely to opt for fifty. These pricing structures can be driven by quantities or sales figures.

Establish Your Payment Terms

With regards to payment terms, it is okay initially to ask for payment in advance. However, further down the track it tends to be detrimental for the distributors. Thirty days or thirty days to the end of the month is generally considered acceptable; I would not generally recommend going over this. With one of my clients, I have added a clause which I think is very effective. Basically it states, 'Our payment terms are thirty days. In case of delay in payment, we reserve the right to change payment terms'. In this way, if you're dealing with a distributor you know is slow to pay, you can revert the payment terms back to payment in advance. While there are some differences between countries, usually these terms are accepted everywhere. French businesses are required by law to pay their suppliers within sixty days. Otherwise, they can encounter a fine of 375,000 Euros.

Italians will always tend to negotiate payment terms that are quite long so be sure to be firm and stick to your guns. As small businesses, we cannot afford to put our financial wellbeing at risk.

The Question of Exclusivity

What should you do with regards to exclusivity? As a general rule, I usually recommend that you don't give exclusivity to anybody whatsoever. In the exporting industry, the biggest mistake I have seen a small business make is to give exclusivity to a distributor for a period of three years in a number of European countries and in return get no sales.

Generally speaking, in Europe it is very rare for a distributor to be a top performer in every single European country. If someone comes to you claiming that they're currently operating in all European countries, be on your guard. Even if you're dealing with a large multinational company and they talk big numbers to you and make it sound amazing, still ensure that you are careful not to 'put all your eggs into one basket'. Large multinationals may have a specific priority one day and the next day there is a major shift in priority. If you are no longer their priority, they won't look after you. Consequently, my blanket recommendation is for no exclusivity. As a small business owner, this will offer you a good safeguard to help you to mitigate the risk of exporting in your business.

Now, I am not suggesting that you cannot appoint someone as a sole distributor for a couple of months (or even for a year) in order to give them plenty of time to become familiar with your business and build up the confidence to develop your sales. The good thing about this arrangement is that if something does go wrong with the relationship, you have the freedom to appoint another distributor relatively quickly. You retain control and are able to call the shots.

If, for any reason, you have no choice and are forced to enter into an exclusivity agreement with a distributor, it is vital for you to contain it by specifying some limitations on the exclusivity agreement. What I mean by this statement is to give the agreement a timeline and some context. For example, you might settle on an arrangement for exclusivity for a one-year period for a specific industry within a specific territory, with the proviso that the exclusivity ceases if, at the end of a one-year period, X$ sales objectives have not been achieved.

Nevertheless, there is rarely any valid reason to give exclusivity, except if the distributor or client comes to you with a multi-million Euros deal right here and right now and you are happy with this arrangement. Negotiation involves giving and receiving, so if you ever give exclusivity make sure you receive enough from the other party to cover the risk.

25

Generating Initial Sales Leads

While working with small business owners in my exporting business, I have found that what works amazingly well is to start to generate some interest for their product in the market while attempting to engage potential distributors. By doing this, you are able to prove to the distributors that your product is validated by the market. This is also a good method for ensuring that your distributors are the right ones for your business.

To give you an example, we recently had to recruit a distributor for the German market for one of my clients. We were targeting a specific industry niche which we were aware our client had developed a solution for. We found out that this specific industry niche held their annual industry trade show during my scheduled trip to Germany that year so I was available to meet all of the potential distributors at the same time. This gave me the opportunity to better understand their problems and gauge their level of interest. From there, I then had the opportunity to talk to the distributors positioned within this niche and say: 'XYZ client of yours is interested in our product. Would you like to test it for them? If you were distributing it for them, who do you think would buy from you?' When I discuss this situation with potential distributors I am always very open about whom I've met with previously; doing so causes your credibility to skyrocket in the distributor's eyes. So, I strongly recommend you conduct your campaign in a similar manner.

A good way to get your foot in the door with potential customers is to offer a 'try and buy' option. If you're already aware that potential users are ready to buy your product you obviously don't want to give it away – in this case, of course, you should sell it. However, sometimes it may be hard for a newcomer to enter the market when their competitors' products are well established. In this situation, you might like to experiment with different options such as:

- A try-and-buy trial for three months. If they like your product, you then invoice them at the end of the three-month period. If they don't like it, then they simply return the product to you.
- You invoice the trial product and send it to them with the offer to credit the price of the trial product on their next order.

All of these terms need to be clearly articulated before the trial product is shipped to the potential customer. It is critical for you to get feedback from these potential customers. You need to find out what they did or didn't like about your product. Aim to get a clear idea of their perception of your product; it will be helpful for you in building your understanding of the market. I definitively recommend creating a feedback form that you deliver to them as part of the trial. You need to get them to commit in writing to providing feedback at the end of the trial period; write a mini agreement that you get them to sign before the trial commences.

If you find that one of your new clients likes your product, you can then ask them if they'd be willing to refer your products to others and write a testimonial for you. This is a very powerful strategy when it comes to marketing to that specific market. Companies will be more likely to buy from you if they know that one of their colleagues or competitors also bought the product and liked it. You need to reward this new client in some way and build your relationship with them. Often, they will become your future allies when it comes to introducing and trialling new products.

Lobby Opinion Leaders and Influencers within Your Industry

Within any industry, there are always a number of influencers or key opinion leaders who have a significant impact on prevailing trends and market share. In the preparation phase of your exporting journey (covered in Section One of this book), I suggested that you should contact some leaders in your field and ask them if you could interview them down the track. Now is the time for you to put this strategy into action! When it comes to making a decision to buy your product, your target market is paying close attention to opinion leaders and influencers. So, get in touch with these key people, especially if you're finding it challenging to generate initial leads. They will help you to better understand if there are any issues with your product and the reason why it's currently not popular in the marketplace.

Depending on your industry, key people of influence can have very different profiles. I will give you several examples to help you identify who could be an influencer within your industry. In the medical sector, it's very easy to identify them; they are often the doctor or professor who are the specialists in a specific discipline where your product is used. They often talk at congresses or hold positions on committees. In the digital space, you may find a blogger who is influential in a particular space as he or she regularly writes reviews of products. Alternatively, this person may be a television presenter or a celebrity. As a small business owner, it may be hard to reach them or commit significant funds to hire them. Sometimes, it can also be a matter of finding the right journalist who regularly publishes articles about your product range; in this case, they might be the person of influence you need to connect with.

When you start exporting to a country, you usually won't have a strong sales track record in that particular country. For this reason, having support from a local key opinion leader will give you an extra advantage in convincing new clients to make the switch to your product.

26

Doing Business with Multinational Companies

Small businesses sometimes find it confronting and feel daunted trying to sell to large multinationals. Of course, it can be a challenge to be a supplier to a large business; I will explain why later in this chapter. However, as a small business owner, there is no reason for you to feel intimidated when approaching a large multinational company. Throughout my career, I have found that these companies are often very clear about what they are not doing well and are quite open to suggestions from small businesses.

When I first started working for IBM in Paris as a young sales representative, I attended a one-year sales training program in Belgium at the IBM European Training Centre. This training was very comprehensive and tough, and I've since found it very useful in all areas of my professional life. After a few years at IBM, I undertook another excellent sales training program which taught me how to deal with buyers and the purchasing process. During the lunch break, I had the opportunity to have a chat with the trainer and found out that her training company was contracted by IBM to deliver this training. Her business had only employed three people; it was a micro-business. I was amazed that such a small business could be engaged to work for such a large corporation. In this case, IBM had simply recognised that its sales representatives were dealing quite well with IT departments, but huge areas of improvement were needed when it came to dealing with buyers.

Small Businesses Helping Multinational Companies

There is plenty of room for small businesses to deal with large corporations if they are able to meet a need, solve a problem or fill a gap. You just have to find out what that issue is. Furthermore, large corporations are not always able to move quickly enough and they recognise the value of fast moving, agile small businesses that are experts in their field and can help them achieve their objectives.

On several occasions, I have been specifically mandated to introduce a small business to a large European company. In some cases, as a small business owner, the solution you are offering is very niche and your target market is a handful of large multinationals. In that case, there is often no need for a distributor to act on your behalf. It may even be counter-productive to have one. To give you an example: one of my French clients is involved in manufacturing a material for the construction industry. In the European market, he sells directly to a large number of multinationals. His material has unique properties and is eco-friendly. When he entered the Australian market, he didn't consider it was necessary to change his selling strategy. We approached Australian subsidiaries of his European clients directly, as well as other large Australian businesses. We were contacted by an Australian importer, but as we'd already made direct contact with large clients there was no point in giving a margin to a distributor when the Australian clients were happy to import directly from the French manufacturer. In this case, the volume was large enough to justify this approach.

On many occasions, I have been mandated to test the interest of large multinationals in a specific technology. In some cases, small businesses have been responsible for developing a breakthrough technology or a new scientific process. Once again, this new technology or process may only be useful for a handful of companies. In this case, Europe is often a great market as it is home to a large number of multinationals who are always looking to improve their productivity and protect their leadership status. If you have what they need, they will listen to what you have to offer. You need to be clear in your own mind about which division in the company has the issue and could benefit from your assistance. Or you may want to test a given multinational company's interest in your technology, in which case you need to have a clear understanding of the person from whom you need feedback. The more specific you are about what you're looking for, the easier it is for anybody working within a large multinational to refer you to the right person. In the worst-case scenario, if you don't have any contacts at all in the multinational company you are targeting, you will have to explain to a receptionist who you're looking for. So, the best way to shorten this process is to be very specific.

Within my business, Exportia, I will sometimes have a list of contacts in a few of these European companies and at other times I won't. I always find it beneficial to have a clear picture of who I need to speak to. People are much more helpful when they clearly understand what and who you are looking for.

Approaching Multinational Companies

What is the best way for SMEs to approach multinationals in order to do business with them? In the past few years, a number of programs have been developed by large European multinationals specifically designed to target start-up companies. These programs are often part of the large corporation's R&D strategy or of their overall innovation program. What often happens is that European expatriates throughout the world are mandated to identify eligible start-ups for these programs. The partnership arrangement the multinational company is offering can be quite broad, such as:

- co-development of intellectual property
- capital investment
- involvement in your board of directors
- integration of your product offering into their product range.

Before applying for one of these programs, I recommend that you carefully assess what their priorities are in terms of investment. Multinational companies have usually clearly identified a number of key areas where they are looking for solutions in order to solve specific issues (e.g. high energy costs) or to improve their service to their customers. If your solution falls within their list of priorities, you will save yourself time and have a greater chance of success.

In my exporting business, I regularly come across a range of different programs offered by multinationals in the ICT, environment and transport sectors. A few years ago, I decided to introduce a client of mine to one of these programs and we found that it was well articulated at a high level. However, later on, we realised that the objective my client was seeking – getting the multinational to adopt his product as a tool for their sales representatives to use (which would have resulted in very large sales for his business) – was difficult to achieve. The reason was that not every business unit within the corporation was fully informed about his product and so it seemed they had no incentive to use it.

If you do decide to get involved in these types of programs, you need to be very clear about what you want to get out of them and ensure that what you are asking for is feasible. Likewise, it is important to find out how it could help you to meet your objectives, both in the short term and over a longer timeframe. Often, these offerings can seem very glamorous and sound like a great opportunity for a small business, but large multinational companies tend to take their time and then change direction abruptly due to budget cuts. So, make sure you don't allocate all of your resources into one avenue and that this particular program is not your only opportunity. Nevertheless, if you're in the right place at the right time, leveraging these types of programs can be fantastic. If you're thinking of selling your business down the track, it is also a great way to give your business exposure to potential buyers. Large multinationals are constantly on the lookout for small businesses to buy.

If the multinationals you are targeting do not offer these types of programs, then you're going to have to resort to the traditional sales approach. Obviously, an introduction to someone working in the company will make your life easier. Think about anyone in your extended network who may be able to provide an introduction for you. If there's no one who can help you, you're going to have to identify all of the stakeholders involved in the decision-making process yourself. Don't focus your attention solely on the purchasing department. Consider all of the personnel who are likely be consulted by the buyer and who would need to be convinced that your solution could make a difference to their business. Approach them and ask them about their needs, their challenges and what their top priorities are.

In some sectors, you will need to partner with companies already supplying to these large multinationals in order for you to be able to supply to them. If you get knocked back by a buyer, don't immediately accept the situation; it is very normal. Some purchasing departments are attempting to reduce the number of their suppliers to achieve more economies of scale, so it may be difficult for them to justify purchasing your product if you don't have a very large range. In that case, ask them who their current suppliers are in your category and who is the best contact person.

The best example of this situation is within the aeronautics sector where small businesses have no other way to approach multinationals other than through partnering with Tier 2 suppliers. On several occasions, Airbus management have confirmed to me that there is no point in smaller businesses wasting time trying to work directly with their company.

27

European Trade Show Fundamentals

When dealing with small companies, I often encounter business owners who are disappointed with the outcome of an industry trade show. My conclusion is always the same: they have not devoted sufficient time and resources to properly prepare for the event. I regularly suggest to my clients that they launch their product range at major European trade shows. In Europe, trade shows are a powerful business marketing venue; they provide an opportunity to meet other players within your industry and to gain a deeper understanding of the European market.

When you're preparing to enter the European market, attending a trade show as a visitor can be a useful fact-finding exercise. It may also be useful if you are targeting a new industry vertical. You may decide to visit a trade show to gather some market information and quickly identify who the key players are in your industry, to generate leads, or to approach a distributor.

Attending an industry trade show is a costly exercise; however, in some industries and/or countries it is an essential requirement for entering the marketplace. For example, in

Germany your business won't be taken seriously if you don't exhibit at the trade show for your industry. Of course, it is important to base your trade show selection on the demographics of your target market. It's easy to check out the trade show's website for statistics about visitor profiles (e.g. general public, professionals) and their country of origin.

European trade shows offer businesses a range of different levels of market exposure: they may have a regional or national focus, or they can be European or internationally-based events. International trade shows are often only held every two years, so make sure that you check the dates before making a commitment to attend.

It's important to note that just having a booth at a European trade show does not mean that you'll be able to achieve guaranteed sales. Over the years I have spent attending trade shows in Europe on behalf of my Australians clients, I have developed a number of tools to automate the process and to share the various tasks among my clients' team. I use the same tools year after year and strive to constantly refine and improve them.

Selecting the Best Trade Show for Your Business

Before making the decision about which industry trade shows are best suited to your business, you first need to be very clear about your objectives and have a well-defined idea about the final outcome you hope to achieve.

Generally speaking, what you want to know is whether the profile of the trade show's visitors and exhibitors corresponds to the particular market you are targeting. Is it truly a European trade show or does it only have local reach? Where do the majority of the visitors come from? Is it orientated towards business to business (B2B) or business to consumers (B2C)? In addition, you need to find out if the distributors you are targeting are going to be exhibiting at the trade show.

In some cases, I will send junior staff to regional trade shows to represent my client's brand and to assist retail shops to raise brand awareness. This is useful when you have two layers of distribution: a wholesaler selling to retailers. The wholesaler may not have the time and resources to promote your brand so you may have to do so yourself.

Benefits of Attending Trade Shows

There are a range of reasons why it is beneficial for your business to attend a trade show including:

- **If you want to launch a product in a specific country**
  Let's say you are well established in the UK and now want to enter the German market. In this case, attending a national trade show is the way to go. If you've already engaged a distributor in this country, then exhibiting with them will make it cost-effective for both of you. If your objective is to recruit a distributor or additional exhibitor, then you should exhibit in your own right.

- **If you wish to recruit new European-wide distributors or business partners**
  All the European distributors visit the European trade shows to source new products. Of course, the best course of action is to have already identified a number of distributors you would like to meet and invite them to your booth before the trade show commences. Similarly, there may also be some distributors who are keen to approach you.

  If you are very busy at the booth, you need to have a strategy in place to quickly assess if they could be a good distributor for you or not. You would have already defined your ideal distributor's profile, so now you need to formulate three questions that will help you make this decision.

For example:

- Do you sell to resellers or directly to end-users?
- Do you provide after-sales technical support?
- How many sales representatives do you have in your team?

- **If you want to support your distributors to increase their sales**
  Get your distributor to organise a booth at their national trade show and support them on their stand. Be easily recognisable with your company shirt and branding or wear a tag with your company name to demonstrate your support for them.

Of course, you need to ensure that the person you allocate to the stand is able to answer technical questions, and preferably has the necessary European language skills. If not, try to arrange for someone from your distributor's team to assist with interpretation. Another option is to hire a professional interpreter.

Preparing for Trade Shows

To maximise your chances of success at industry trade shows, it's essential that you are very well prepared and have devised a good action plan.

Schedule Meetings in Advance

Download the list of exhibitors from the trade show's website, research relevant businesses in your field (including their core activity, size, and development strategy) and prepare your pitch to them. If they're of particular interest to you, contact them early to introduce your company/product and arrange a meeting. Contact any established clients in the given country to announce your presence at the trade show and propose a meeting during or after the show.

Trade shows in Europe can be huge. Some of these shows have so many halls that, if you're unprepared, you will spend a lot of time roaming around hallways and alleys. For this reason, you need to make sure you organise your meetings schedule three months in advance. This way you can ensure that the people you want to meet have allocated some time to visit you.

For trade shows that have a European or international exposure, be aware that in most cases, all of the European distributors will have made plans to visit their suppliers while they are there. So, if you are targeting a specific manufacturer, make sure you arrange a meeting time with them three to six months in advance.

Tell the World!

Inform your own network of your attendance at a trade show using a specially created email signature. Likewise, use social media and newsletters to advertise your presence. As part of your exhibitor's kit, you will usually receive a trade show logo that you can upload to your website and use on any digital media.

To increase your exposure, you can also place an advertisement in the national trade magazine and inform professionals within your industry or the general public about your presence at the trade show and where they can find you. There will usually be an option to write your company and product description in English and in the local language on the trade show's website. I advise you to do both as it will help you gain better visibility. In addition, pay attention to product categories to make sure your booth is in a prominent position when visitors are looking for your product.

A Professional-Looking Booth is Crucial for Success

Europeans use trade shows as an essential strategy for conducting business, and so some of the booths you'll observe will be amazing! For this reason, trade shows offer an ideal opportunity for you to create and promote your brand image to a wide audience.

Devote some time and money to having a professional booth at the trade show – put some care into this exercise. If you sell a premium high-tech product, your booth needs to look premium as well. I know that small businesses are sometimes reluctant to invest in a booth. This is a shame because a modular, flexible booth is a great long-term investment as it can be used over a number of years. The main criteria is flexibility so that it can be adapted to various floor space shapes or sizes. Your business branding may change over time. Therefore, ensure your signage is removable so it can be easily changed.

Make your booth visible and attractive by organising live product demonstrations, video presentations, or samples giveaways. Talk to your clients in their own language and consider producing a selection of marketing collateral such as samples, brochures, and banners that will support your product demonstrations at the show. Prepare them well in advance as you may realise that some tools need to be translated or adapted. Trust me – it will make a big difference if you can provide information in French to a French person!

Maximise Exhibitors' Packages

Exhibition organisers offer a number of marketing options that you will need to consider. It is particularly useful for you to be in the visitor's program, particularly if you have a new product and you can showcase it in the new product section.

If you have a significant innovation, try and find out if you can apply for an innovation award. This is a great opportunity to attract attention to your business. You will achieve a better outcome if you apply for an award if you already have a distributor that can leverage it for you. It will definitely help if you can lodge the application form in the local language; ask your distributor to help you with this task.

Leveraging Trade Show Attendance

Always keep in mind that the purpose of attending any industry trade show is to generate leads for your business. For this reason, your approach should be sales-focused so you can leverage your investment.

Be Efficient when Collecting Leads

It is important to collect contact details for anyone visiting your booth. The most efficient way I've found for doing this is to use an old-fashioned notebook where you staple business cards you have collected and write the person's enquiry and what step you need to take with this contact beside each card. At the end of every day (or as you go), you then rate the priority level for each contact – one, two, three, etc. I know this seems quite basic but it really works! It's very helpful because when you arrive back home, you are already aware of who you should get in touch with as soon as possible.

Depending on the particular style of the trade show, there are much more high-tech methods you can use to collect information. For example, you can hire badge scan systems. You can also use an iPad or tablet applications to scan badges or business cards and capture contact details.

If you are targeting the general public, organising a lucky draw, asking people to sign your visitor book or offering them the opportunity to sign up to your newsletter are other good ways of collecting contact information.

Strive for Continuous Improvement

At the end of each exhibit day, write down all of the things you've identified for improvement at the next trade show. For example, you may have observed interesting innovations and ideas from other exhibitors. Likewise, you may have realised that you need more or better quality brochures, or that you should offer more catering options to visitors This list of things will help you to improve your performance at future trade shows.

Follow-up with Your Leads

You are now back home ready to relax after an exhausting week and feeling happy that your task is completed. Sorry to bring up the bad news, but there is still a lot to be done!

At this point, the work starts with nurturing the new leads you have found. The first thing you need to do is to send a thank-you email to all of the people who visited your booth. Generally speaking, this should be done within the first few days after the trade show. It can be a generic email where the text is the same for everyone. The text can be as simple as: 'Thank you for visiting us at the XYZ trade show. Please do not hesitate to contact us if you have any enquiries'. That gives you time to follow up every enquiry one by one – an action that will help to build your credibility. If anyone has an urgent enquiry, this makes it easy for them to write to you.

The next step is to provide a personalised response to the priority number one leads, then number two and then number three. At this point in time, you'll be glad you have rated them on the spot. Then you can get straight into it. Send them your newsletter or regular personalised emails just so they remember you (note that they need to have opted in to your email list). Then it is up to you to organise follow-up visits to convert these leads into sales opportunities.

Analyse the Outcome of Your Trade Show Participation

Finally, it is essential to measure your return on investment for the trade show. This does not need to be a complicated process. You can simply record your answers to such questions as: Did you benefit from your trade show participation? What are the positive outcomes (e.g. sales increase, number of leads)? What could be improved? How? Did your participation meet your expectations?

This analysis will help you define your strategy for future trade shows. For example, should you attend other similar trade shows or should you try something with a different target audience? Do you want to return to the same show next year? It is important to understand that you need to be present at these events year after year to be able to gain traction and make yourself known in the marketplace. Persistence is key in the European market. If you are willing to devote the necessary time and resources, you will see your exporting activities progress each year and gradually more doors will open for you.

The Power of a One-Day Visit to a Trade Show

Last year, I conducted a lead generation campaign in the German market to launch my client's product in a new industry vertical – one that they had never previously worked in before in Europe. As we started identifying the major manufacturers in this industry, we quickly noticed that all of them were exhibiting at a national congress. As I happened to be visiting Germany at the time of the congress, I convinced my client that I should spend a day there. We then organised a meeting plan and called the relevant companies. All the targeted companies were informed that I would be present on that day and available to meet with them. Rather than being a random company calling them and emailing them from Australia, I was able to meet all of the targeted twenty companies in a day. Most of them agreed to receive more information from us and I learnt which of my client's products would fit their industry. A few months after the show, my client and I visited two factories. And six months after the show, the first order arrived!

The other great outcome is that I was able to quickly identify that they all bought my client's category of product from one distributor. They were all satisfied with this distributor as they'd been receiving good service. At the time of writing this book, this particular distributor is trialling my client's product and he seems quite happy with it. As soon as we engage them, I will send him the list of leads that I collected during the congress in Germany. Since all of the leads on this list are already his clients, he will already know the people I met and what product(s) they are interested in. See how much you can achieve in a one-day visit to a trade show if you are well prepared!

SECTION FIVE

....

Achieving Sustainable Export Sales

28

The Foundations for Sustainable Export Sales

One common misconception I often come across with small businesses is that once the distributor has been appointed, they think the job is done. However, this is exactly where things can go wrong and so it should be where you focus the majority of your attention. Distributors are also busy running their own businesses and need to ensure your offer works for them. If it's difficult for them to generate initial sales for your product, they will soon lose interest. The process needs to quickly yield results for them. For this reason, in the early stages, you need to be by the distributor's side, constantly monitoring what is happening.

If you've appointed a wholesaler who conducts business by means of a large product catalogue, you have to be realistic about how much time they are going to devote to selling your product. If it's too hard for them, they will switch to another product. To give you an example, I was able to introduce my client's product range to a major French wholesaler. This wholesaler has the largest list of clients in France and is the leading

French business within that market. My client's product was quite technical so we were aware that the arrangement wouldn't work without direct lead generation activity from them. The wholesaler's four sales representatives visit hundreds of retail shops throughout the year. They spend a large amount of their time preparing their catalogue and price updates. Whenever they visit a shop, they review an extensive range and look at broad turnover figures. The wholesaler did not have the skills (or the time or even the motivation) to train their retailers about the technical details of my client's products. The majority of their work involves providing retailers with a merchandised shop concept and stocking the products; they are like a marketing machine!

Now, consider this scenario from my client's perspective. If their product is to be sold by a retailer, the manager of the shop and his team must be trained because they need to understand what the product is all about. Likewise, the people at the workshop need to be trained on how they can install it. Referring back to the wholesaler's sales representative, he has thirty minutes to one hour available to visit a retailer; therefore, it is highly unlikely that he will spend this time on just one product.

So clearly, once you have appointed a distributor, the work has only just started! You need to treat your distributors in the same way as your clients. Remember, they are your clients and you're competing for their attention, their time and the space they will allocate for your business in their catalogue and marketing collateral.

Dealing with Under-Performing Distributors

What can you do if the distributor you've appointed is not performing to a sufficiently high standard for your business? Managing a distributor who is under-performing is always tricky and should follow a pre-established procedure. It is important to clearly define this process from the start of the engagement. Generally speaking, the best way to handle this situation is to establish minimum targets; even the smallest volume can save you down the track from working with a distributor who is not able to deliver any results for you.

The other method is to restrict the agreement to a limited period. It's usually hard to limit it to only six months as it is difficult for a distributor to achieve results within this short timeframe – a year is more realistic. At the end of the year, conduct a review and then, at this point, you can make your final decision.

29

Instructing Your Indirect Salesforce

You've spent months carefully selecting the best European distributor for your product. You have negotiated and finalised the trading terms. This is the honeymoon period! Now you need to quickly train your distributor's sales team.

Training Your Distributor's Sales Team

Depending on your distribution model, you may need to train the sales team for several levels of service and for different types of audiences. For example:

- If your distribution model is composed of a wholesaler that sells to a network of retailers, you will need to train the wholesaler's sales representatives and the retailer's team.

- If your distribution model involves a B2B distributor who targets end-users, then your distributor's sales team is your target audience.

It is often the case that, following the training session, a stock order will often follow. It's usually a good sign if the distributor shows a lot of interest in training their team as it demonstrates how serious they are about your product. For some distributors, removing their salesforce from the field for a day to attend a training program is a day when they won't generate new sales. Consequently, if they have made plans to organise training for their sales reps, you can feel reassured that they are committed to your product.

For a small business with limited resources, this investment in training needs to be very strategic, especially if your distributor has more than 100 sales representatives. You need to carefully consider your resources and the best way of allocating them. This is a case of 'betting on the right horse'; these distributors are your early adopters so you need to be able to clearly identify them.

There are different ways for you to get started. Depending on the distributor's size and how their organisation is structured, it's usually a good practice to consult with the product managers in charge of your product category or the head of your product division. Arrange to have a conversation with them to find out what they think is the best plan for launching and growing your product sales. You aren't yet familiar with your distributor's sales team so you need to quiz them regarding who is their best salesperson for your product. They know their team well so they will be able to tell you. In the high-tech space, you may also want to find out who is the most technically savvy.

National distributors with a very large national spread can also be a challenge for a small business with limited resources when it comes to training a very large team. It is justifiable to ask them if you can conduct regional training. With sufficient notice, teams can get together and you can train twenty to thirty representatives at a time. It will save you time and travel expenses. You may also like to experiment with training a couple of regions first to test the level of adoption of your product. Once you've validated this approach, you can then replicate this format in other regions. You can also seek advice about the most dynamic regions or the largest regions you should target first. Frequently, it is all about personalities – when you initially presented your product to this distributor you may have found that one or two people were really enthusiastic about your product. These people are also very good allies for you inside your distributor's organisation; they can guide you through what can, at times, be a tricky maze.

While you're training your indirect salesforce, it's a good idea to be reviewing all of the attendees to find out who might be your future best sales representatives. In any audience, you will always find a few people who will ask more questions. They will often ask questions about specific client's case studies and what happened with them. These sales representatives may be the ones who will work hardest to sell your product.

While you're conducting your training program, it is also a good time to gain as much intelligence as possible about your market. Different regions have different types of industries and people. Ask the representatives in the room to fill you in with more details about their clients.

It goes without saying that you really need to deliver the training to the distributor's sales team in their own language. If you don't have the requisite language skills yourself, hire the services of a professional interpreter for the occasion. You might also request for one person from the distributor's team to do the interpreting for you. Make sure you organise this well in advance of the training date. It is critical to make sure you communicate your message clearly to your training audience. Otherwise, it will be a waste of time, money and energy for everyone.

Finally, in order for them to stay motivated, you need to commit to regularly re-training them. The second training

session may be conducted through e-learning programs including online videos.

Optimal Format for Your Sales Training Programs

Face-to-face training is usually the most effective option for any
sales raining programs. Get your distributor's sales representatives in a room and train them on the product itself, on how
they should pitch it and on who is the best customer profile
for your products. By doing this, you can avoid having them
try to sell your product to the wrong target market which, in
turn, creates the perception that your product is hard to sell. As
a small business owner, this is particularly important because
you're not going to be operating by their side. Consequently,
they need to be trained to look for the easy wins so that they
get quick results and stay motivated.

Share Your Company Profile

First of all, you need to introduce your company to the
distributor's sales representatives. Ensure that you share such
background information as where your company originated,
as well as why this product was invented in the first place.
Sales representatives love to tell the stories behind a product.
For example, I am currently helping a client of mine to commercialise a safety product to protect workers in different
industries. The product was invented by engineers from the
medical device industry. We trained about a hundred representatives and explained to them where the company and product
originated. Since then, I have visited a number of clients with
the representatives we trained and I often hear the information
about the medical background we conveyed during their training program used as a differentiator.

Explain Your Product's Technical Features

After sharing your company story, training on the actual product will obviously take place. This is all about the technical features of your products and I usually find that my clients have no problem explaining these facts. Send someone who has enough technical skills to explain your product range inside out to deliver this training.

Demonstrate How to Sell Your Product

Another important area to train your distributor's sales representatives in is the 'how to sell' aspect of your product. You need to explain what the best conditions are for selling your product, including which type of clients they should target. You have to help them to make sure the deals are signed as quickly as possible so they can get out and start selling. You need to be able to guide them to the 'low hanging fruit' by pointing out to them who the early adopters of your product are likely to be. If they try to target clients who are the wrong audience for your product, they will find it too difficult and quickly lose interest.

You also need to show them how to demonstrate the product to a client. If you have a good 'return on investment' story available it will also be a very powerful resource for them to use.

Allocate Time for Questions

Plenty of time should be allocated during the training program for questions. You will learn a lot from questions your training audience asks. Quiz them in order to gain as much insight as possible about their 'pain points' and the areas they currently find challenging.

Provide Sales Packs

Ideally, at the end of the training session, you should provide every sales representative with a sales pack to take with them. It is important to leverage their enthusiasm at the end of the training program.

Obviously, a brochure should be the bare minimum to be included in the sales pack you give to your indirect salesforce. It can be very powerful to collate new customers' testimonials and turn them into compelling case studies. Of course, the best option is to collect case studies from your export market. However, if you're just starting out, then simply use case studies from your domestic market and translate them into the appropriate languages. They will still have a lot of impact on your market. Case studies make it easy for sales reps to showcase your product and to demonstrate that others who have purchased your product are happy with it. If you have already sold to a European customer, I strongly recommend using this customer as a reference.

In addition, user manuals in the correct language should also be incorporated in the sales kit, as well as a document that lists your recommended retail price or recommended selling price. If you've done any advertising or had articles printed in European magazines, be sure to include them in the sales pack as well. In addition, any industry awards are very appropriate to include, as are any demonstration videos that you have had voiced-over or produced by a native speaker.

The sales representatives will need to have your product with them when they are visiting clients. Depending on the cost of your product, if you can afford to give it away then that's obviously perfect. However, if this is too costly for your company, you can bundle free samples with a stock order.

Training Retailers

In terms of selecting the best retailers for your exporting activities, you may want to select the top ten retailers who have the best technical profile for your product. Likewise, those retailers who provide the best customer service and are clearly the most motivated are usually a good pick. You also need to identify the retailers that sell the biggest volume in your product category. I recommend that you work closely with your wholesaler to identify these retailers.

Another possible solution is to train them during the annual event organised by wholesalers; this can often be your best option. Once a year, it is usual practice for the wholesaler to request their manufacturers to train their network of resellers. This is a great opportunity for you to train several retailers at once. When it comes to training retailers, the only other option is to train them at their shop – a process that can be quite time consuming but works relatively well.

For retailers, the most important consideration is training their shop sales representatives. In this case, training is not relevant without having point-of-sales marketing and merchandising in place. It makes sense to have your merchandising installed at the same time as conducting the in-shop training. Make it easy for the in-shop sales representatives to have a simple explanation of your product at hand when demonstrating it to the client.

A few years ago we developed a poster, with an explanation of our client's product, to be placed inside shops. The aim of this exercise was to help customers with decision-making by clarifying the various steps involved so as to give them confidence that the product was the right fit for them. It is difficult to sell a high-tech product through retail so your explanations have to be visual and as simple as possible to comprehend.

Forget about using long textual explanations in a retail environment; it needs to be immediate and easy to understand.

I have found that a good approach with European wholesalers is for them to hold the merchandising material and to dispatch it to each retailer with the delivery of a stock order.

30

Engaging Sales Agents Versus Hiring Your Own Salesforce

Before launching into your exporting operations in Europe, you need to first weigh up which is the better option for your business: engaging sales agents or hiring your own salesforce in Europe.

Reasons for Engaging a Sales Agent

When you don't have a local presence in Europe, it's hard to keep an eye on your distributor's sales representatives. In addition, it makes it difficult to ensure that they are going to always keep your product high in their priority list. For this reason, in some cases, I have found it beneficial to recruit a sales agent for my clients.

Often non-Europeans are not aware of what is involved in hiring employees in Europe. First of all, you need to create a company to be able to employ someone. Then you need to understand local laws and the different types of employment contracts. This situation is currently undergoing change within Europe; however, traditionally, employment contractual arrangements are quite constraining for the employer. There's a big difference between hiring employees in France and Australia. For example, it is much less risky for a small business to hire staff in Australia than it is in France. In France, it is very hard for an employer to dismiss someone if they don't perform well, particularly if there is conflict and the disgruntled employee tries to take you to court. Any employment contract is regulated under French law, so imagine having to deal with translation costs and lawyer fees to manage the worst-case scenario!

For a small business owner, managing employees when you are not physically present in the country can be quite risky and costly. A few years ago, one of my clients experienced this problem, even though they were an Australian company and were involved in hiring someone based in the UK where both legal systems have some similarities and English is the common language.

I always recommend that small businesses look for the most flexible, low-risk option for exporting. During the initial stages of your exporting operation, you should always have the ability to get out fast if you need to. When your turnover grows and you become well established, you can then consider moving to the next stage and hiring your own salesforce in Europe through a local subsidiary.

You need to be aware that even large European companies opt to have quite flexible company structures in several European countries. I know of a major German manufacturer who has an arrangement with their French distributor to be their representative in France. So, they actually have a French company but it is managed by their distributor. European manufacturers (even large ones) also often use sales agents in their own country or in other European countries instead of recruiting their own salesforce.

Advantages of Engaging a Sales Agent

The main benefit for small businesses in appointing sales agents is the territory coverage they offer. By engaging the services of a sales agent, you can ensure your product receives broad national coverage. Your sales agent will spend time visiting customers and will talk to your distributor's sales team every day. They can develop your network of local distributors or target end-users. They will also be available to respond to day-to-day enquiries about your product, which will free you up to focus on more strategic activities within this market (i.e. your relationship with key accounts)

Generally speaking, sales agents are paid commissions only, so dealing with them is low risk for you. However, if you need to discontinue a contract, you will have to pay an indemnity to your agent. In a few European countries, there are regulations associated with engaging sales agents. These outlines the obligations of the company appointing the agent and of the agent themselves. It's important that you find out your legal obligations before recruiting a sales agent for your business. For example, a sales agent should represent several companies. If the agent you're about to recruit represents you alone, you are at risk that they are entitled to request to be requalified as one of your employees. This then means that you would have to create a company and employ them as a staff member, entitling them to the same social benefits as a regular employee. So, at the outset, make sure you are not the only company they are working for.

I recommend that you check first with a local European lawyer about the different risks associated with appointing a sales agent for your business before finalising their engagement contract.

Locating Sales Agents

Over the years, I have tried several approaches to recruiting sales agents for my clients, including placing advertisements on sales agents' websites. Generally speaking, I have not found advertising on websites particularly effective; however, it may differ from country to country.

For me, the most successful strategy is always word of mouth. Quite frankly, I have found that talking to local people in your industry is the best approach to doing business in Europe. Obviously, it means that you won't be able to achieve results if you don't have a good understanding of the local players. You need to have a local European network in place in order to be able to cross-check information.

The best source of information about sales agents will be your distributors. Your distributor's sales representatives regularly work with sales agents. If you find that within your industry your distributors never see a sales agent and never work with them, then working with a sales agent may not be the best option for your business. If they do, then ask them which ones have the most experience working with your product category. Ask them which sales agents they find best to work with and are likely to offer you the most support. After some time, if your product has sufficient traction, sales agents will contact you as word about your business spreads.

Another good strategy is to approach other manufacturers who deal with non-competitive products and ask them for their advice. This can easily be done at a trade show or over the phone.

The Terms of Engagement

Before you appoint a sales agent for your business, see what you can afford in terms of percentage of sales. It may vary between seven to ten per cent (or more) of sales depending on your product and industry. I suggest that it's a good idea to start with a trial period as it offers you an easy way out if you're not satisfied with an agent's services. Remember that reporting to you will be more limited than if they were your own employees, since they are running their own business. Generally speaking, I have found that regular phone calls and emails work better than reporting processes which tend to be laborious and time consuming.

Are Sales Agents the Best Option for Every European Union Country?

In order to determine whether or not hiring a sales agent is your best option for every European Union country you will need to make a lot of enquires, including talking to your distributors and end-clients. In my experience, I find it usually depends on the country and then, within each country, on the specific industry.

In Germany, independent sales agents don't always have a good reputation. In this case, both distributors and clients think that it is preferable to establish a German company and hire your own staff. However, this should not be taken as a general rule as I have seen excellent agents operating in German high-tech industries.

In France, engaging the services of an independent sales agent is quite common. However, your decision will really depend upon the industry, as the quality of agents differs industry by industry.

In Italy, sales agents are relatively common because distribution networks can sometimes be quite dispersed.

The best advice I can give you regarding sales agents is to ask, ask and ask. Word-of-mouth is a wonderful resource!

31

Maintaining Your Export Sales Momentum

Now that you have recruited your distributors and possibly also appointed sales agents, you can't just sit back and relax. You have to keep your eye on the ball and ensure you check that the mechanics of your exporting activities are operating smoothly. It is important for you to keep measuring the pulse of your market; even though you have sales agents working for your business, you still need to make contact with your distributor and end-users from time to time to check how things are going. The best way to do that is for you to visit your market and keep in touch with your end-users so that you're aware of what is happening. Meeting your agents and distributors regularly will help you assess how your export sales are progressing. You need to be able to constantly monitor and readjust your exporting strategy.

By now, you will have established minimum sales targets so ensure that you constantly check how you are tracking in your business. Minimum sales targets need to be realistic and you should establish what minimum turnover you want to achieve. At the outset of your exporting operations, you will need to take into account the fact that nobody is familiar with you or your brand. Don't systematically assign sales targets based on your home market experience. In your home market, your brand has some exposure; you already have an established network. Overseas, nobody knows you so don't discourage your indirect salesforce with targets that are too ambitious at the outset. As you build awareness of your product in the European market, you can gradually raise your sales targets.

I strongly recommend that you organise regular check-point meetings where you review how you are tracking against your targets. It's a good idea to conduct some customer visits with your distributor as it can be a great way to quickly find out whether they are targeting the right customers. In addition, it will show you how they sell your product and you will be in a good position to obtain first-hand customer feedback.

Marketing Tools to Support Your Distributors

As a small high-tech business with limited resources and without a local presence in Europe, it can be very challenging to provide adequate support to your overseas distributors. Nevertheless, you need to ensure that your distributors remain engaged and that they keep focusing their efforts to drive sales for your product.

Over the years, I found that any of our clients who were reluctant to have multi-lingual marketing and technical collateral found it much harder to convince overseas distributors' sales teams to market their product. Obviously, the easier you make it for them to promote your product, the better the sales outcomes for your business will be. Generally speaking, if you give European distributors the tools they need in their own language, you will immediately gain their trust and your credibility will rise exponentially.

I'm not only talking here about your regular marketing brochure – it goes without saying that you need to do that. In the high-tech world, it is important to ensure that highly technical and innovative information can be readily understood by a large number of people.

Be Scalable in Multiple Languages

When dealing with the European market, a critical point to remember is that any new marketing project (such as a new catalogue or a new website) should be designed so that it can be easily adapted to multiple languages, and it must also have the capacity to scale. This is particularly the case for your business's website. Inform your web designer from the outset that you want to make provision down the track for a multi-lingual website, so they will need to plan for incorporating accents and specific characters (é; ê; ß; ä, etc.) that make European languages unique. Make sure these characters can be displayed well on your website.

This requirement for scalability into multiple languages implies that any marketing material that you prepare needs to contain the least amount of words possible. For example, if you take a look at the IKEA user manual you will see exactly what I am talking about. From a practical perspective, the fewer words you include in a printed or online document, the cheaper it will be to translate it into multiple languages. Likewise, the fewer words there are the less room there is for misunderstandings. For this reason, I advise you to use drawings and diagrams as much as possible.

If, like most of my clients, you are a non-European company doing business in Europe, you should be aware that your European competitors will already have this aspect of their marketing and sales strategy well covered. Assuming that everybody speaks English is not a good strategy when doing business successfully in Europe.

Using an Online Platform to Streamline your Exporting Activities

How do you share documents with your partners and distributors without having to deal with a heavy email workload? All of this information needs to be readily accessible. Ideally, you want to have all these documents on your website where they are very easy to locate.

If your website doesn't have the capability for this you can use a temporary solution. Don't get discouraged because you think that it's complicated to upload documents to your website. You can use a secure ftp link to folders or, alternatively, you can use 'cloud' solutions. Likewise, you may prefer to use document-sharing solutions via Google Drive and Dropbox and the like. If you want to permit access to only certain categories of people, you will need to have a secured IT system. 'Cloud' solutions are a good option if you are in the process of preparing secure access for partners on your website.

Online is the way to go to maximise your exporting operations and these capabilities need to be planned for when you are initially designing your business website.

REAL-WORLD TOOL: Distributor Reporting Template

When my company first commences working with very large distributors, we use this template to report to their management team. I also use it on other occasions – notably to share with their management team what is happening with sales around the country. Surprisingly, it can be quite normal for the director of a business unit to be unaware of what is happening with your product in different regions. The reason is that he or she is mainly focused on the high-revenue generating products. Therefore, you have to be able to demonstrate to them the beneficial aspects of your product, as well as showcasing all of the good things you are doing in a new export market. This template is a very powerful marketing tool which should be regularly updated on a quarterly or monthly basis.

To download this tool, go the Downloads section of the Exportia website: www.exportia.com.au/downloads

APPENDIX

....

Exporting Client Case Studies

To help you gain a better understanding of the exporting concepts I have discussed in this book, I have documented ten client case studies that my company, Exportia, has been involved with.

CASE STUDY 1: Effenergy – Signing a deal with a major government organisation

Business Profile

Company Name: Effenergy (small business)

Industry: Clean technologies, information technology, transportation

Effenergy develops software solutions which, by combining software development with engineering skills, enable transportation operators to make energy savings.

Past Business Activities

Effenergy had already achieved good results in the UK market and were aware that opportunities were available for them to expand into continental Europe. However, they didn't yet have a clear picture of the key players in either the French or

German markets. Ted (CEO of Effenergy) commissioned us to inform them about the marketplace so they would be in a good position to generate new sales leads.

Major Challenges

The major challenges revolved around the fact that the Effenergy's clients are very large companies (the majority of them are government organisations). This means that the customer's decision cycles are very long and it takes quite a while for a newcomer to be able to identify the right decision makers before the tender process commences. This is particularly the case in countries such as France (and to a lesser extent Germany), where you really need to be able to speak the local language in order to navigate the maze of government departments. The other difficulty involved communicating the project specifications in both French and English.

How Exportia Helped

After identifying the major potential French and German customers, we helped Effenergy to decide on the best options. We then pinpointed the key technical contact people and other specialists in these organisations and gave them a clear brief regarding the information we needed for our client.

As a result, not only did we receive very valuable feedback from each organisation about the likelihood of them buying Effenergy's solution, we also were able to gather information about competitors and the best approach to entering these markets.

We identified an opportunity for Effenergy with a large French semi-public organisation. As a result of my contacts in France, I was able to quickly determine that energy saving was 'top of mind' with high-level stakeholders in this organisation. Since there was a clear need for this product, I could easily pinpoint the right contact person.

We prepared a company presentation in French and I organised an introduction between my client and the French company at their head office in Paris. I also assigned one of my team members based in France to be the French-speaking spokesperson for the French client and to work with the UK-based client team. This created a trust factor for the French company because they had a dedicated contact person with whom they could discuss things in their own language, thus removing possible barriers to closing the deal.

Final Outcome

Effenergy signed a major deal with a very large government organisation, which resulted in a high level of visibility for this Australian business in the European market. This was a major achievement given that the competitive landscape is composed of major multinationals.

CASE STUDY 2: TopElectronics – Negotiating favourable trading terms with distributors

Business Profile

Company Name: TopElectronics (small business)

Industry: Advanced manufacturing

Past Business Activities

TopElectronics had targeted the European marketplace as a priority market for their business and had hired someone based in Europe to look after their exporting activities. However, since the headquarters of the company was located in Australia, Catherine (CEO of TopElectronics) found it hard to get information about the European field and to gain clarity on the best channels for their product. In addition, unfavourable trading terms had been put in place with distributors, which were a risk to TopElectronics.

Major Challenges

The main challenge for TopElectronics involved the need for speedy results and also a method for mitigating their risks. This meant that they needed to find a way of working with the right distributors and establishing profitable trading terms with them.

How Exportia Helped

We researched and interviewed all of the major French distributors to establish a clear picture of this market for our client. We also analysed all of the current agreements and discussions with distributors and proposed a new price list with favourable terms for TopElectronics. We then engaged and trained distributors and conducted sales visits with their sales representatives to customers in both major markets: France and Germany. We also selected and engaged independent sales agents to provide additional support to the distributors' salesforces.

Final Outcome

After receiving an overview of distributors and their activities within the French market, TopElectronics was in a position to make an informed decision to appoint a major national distributor (along with two smaller dynamic distributors) for the French market – a key market for their product. The new trading terms and pricing structure were announced to all of the European distributors. A German network of distributors was then also appointed.

The French market now generates significant revenue for this Australian manufacturing company and the German market is looking promising as well.

CASE STUDY 3: MedicSafe – Using market influencers to help achieve your business goals

Business Profile

Company Name: MedicSafe (small business)

Industry: Medical devices

MedicSafe manufactures a device for cleaning surgical instruments and their main target market is hospitals.

Past Business Activities

MedicSafe had received enquiries from around the world and they were keen to engage distributors in Europe after conducting some due diligence.

Major Challenges

The main challenge for MedicSafe was their small size and the limited funds they had available to allocate to business development in Europe.

How Exportia Helped

We identified, contacted and convinced a major figure within this medical sector to be a supporter of MedicSafe's product. This person was chairing a major association in their sector and had also been accepted by a reputable industry publication to publish a study about the product's performance.

We then presented business profiles of several distributors for MedicSafe to choose their preferred option. The selected distributors were contacted to evaluate their interest and to gather market feedback. We then supported our client as required in smoothing the way for the initial communication with the distributor and helping them to generate sales.

Final Outcome

By identifying and gaining the support of a major influencer in the market for MedicSafe, we were able to assist them to raise their profile. In addition, we helped them to appoint a small-sized distributor who was able to leverage this support in the market and develop sales for them within a six-month timeframe.

CASE STUDY 4: AutoBoost – Adapting your product to the European market

Business Profile

Company name: AutoBoost (medium-sized business)

Industry: Advanced manufacturing, automotive

AutoBoost manufactures an automotive component for vehicles.

Past Business Activities

As the leader in the Australian domestic market, AutoBoost has always developed products that catered to the needs of their local market (including the harsh Australian environment) and relied on their capable sales team.

Major Challenges

When Cliff (CEO of AutoBoost) made the strategic decision to export to Europe, he was aware that the needs of the European markets would be very different from those of the Australian market. The challenge was to make sure that the new product range for export would meet the particular requirements of the European market.

How Exportia Helped

After receiving training from AutoBoost's team, I identified the main manufacturers in the European market and approached them to present this new product to them and collect their feedback and specifications. This process occurred via a series of meetings in Europe and through webinars with Cliff or one of his engineers.

Final Outcome

AutoBoost now has a clear understanding of the needs of European clients and is aware of the functionalities that need to be developed for the different requirements of the European market. After this exercise, it was apparent that these specifications would also be highly appreciated by AutoBoost's Australian clients.

Since we had obtained the technical specifications from one of the European market leaders, this gave AutoBoost the confidence to use this information to adapt their current product and to plan for future product developments.

CASE STUDY 5: FarmTech – Retaining control of your intellectual property

Business Profile

Company Name: FarmTech (small business)

Industry: Machinery; Agriculture

FarmTech manufactures agricultural equipment.

Past Business Activities

FarmTech had been very successful in the US market and did not have sufficient time or resources to focus their attention on both the European market and the US market. So, when a European company contacted them, they were happy to work with them. FarmTech established a licence agreement with this European company whereby they would licence the right to manufacture and distribute FarmTech's product in Europe.

Major Challenges

After a few years, the European partner began to complain about the licence fees, stating that they were left with no margin and so threatened to stop paying it. FarmTech now had more time and resources available to closely examine the European market. FarmTech engaged us to clarify their margin structure and to find out how they could regain control over their business activities.

How Exportia Helped

Exportia initially provided FarmTech with an overview of the European market in terms of potential per country. This, in turn, gave them a good understanding of which country the company should be focusing on. We then selected distributors in the two highest potential countries and interviewed them, requesting feedback about the product range.

The other aspect of the project was to select potential manufacturers in Europe who could work under licence. We identified a number of players in Western and Eastern Europe and made a decision based on the criteria that FarmTech had given us.

Final Outcome

Exportia provided the company with an overview of several distribution models in the European market. This information enabled FarmTech to be better informed when negotiating with European partners about manufacturing and distribution in Europe. If the issue continues to remain unresolved, they now have several alternative avenues for developing business in Europe.

CASE STUDY 6: TechPro – Launching in a new market segment in Europe

Business Profile

Company Name: TechPro (large business)

Industry: Electronics, mining, leisure

TechPro manufactures an electronics device used in the mining and leisure industries.

Past Business Activities

TechPro was already well established in Europe with its own office and staff, plus a European-wide distribution network.

Major Challenges

TechPro is now seeking to expand its business operations outside its traditional distribution network. The Australian head office has made the strategic decision to target the consumer market. The main challenges are that it is a new type of distribution channel which includes much larger retail outlets. The TechPro European team is reluctant to move outside their comfort zone and don't support the move into a new sector. Consequently, they are trying to dissuade the Australian head office by downplaying the size of this market in Europe.

How Exportia Helped

The Exportia team provided TechPro with an overview of the major distribution channels in four key European markets, including their company profile, their industry footprint, their size and their product range. We also introduced

TechPro to a major retail chain which has a footprint in several European countries.

Final Outcome

After we had provided an overview of the consumer distribution channels in four key European countries, TechPro's Australian head office was able to respond to their European team with tangible data about the market. We were even able to demonstrate in our report that competitors were already selling through several large consumer channels in a number of key European markets.

CASE STUDY 7: SoftwareCare – Evaluating the potential of a given European market

Business Profile

Company Name: SoftwareCare (small business)
Industry: Health, IT
SoftwareCare is a software developer for the health industry.

Past Business Activities

SoftwareCare had some presence in the UK and Ireland, but wanted to investigate the potential of the French market in order to expand their business operations.

Major Challenges

The European Union is in charge of most of the regulatory aspects of product compliance within the European medical sector. However, each country has its own specific regulations with regards to private versus public hospitals, and the associated funding systems are also very country-specific. The objective of this project was to assess the feasibility of commercialising

SoftwareCare's solution in France, so one of the main challenges was access to government information and to hospitals.

How Exportia Helped

We were able to provide SoftwareCare with an overview of the funding and the pricing of medical aids in France. In order to assess the potential of the market, we also established a list of their main competitors and what solutions they were offering to hospitals. We then interviewed hospital staff to gather feedback regarding their satisfaction levels with the software solutions they were currently using.

Final Outcome

The Exportia team was able to assess that the French market offered good sales opportunities for SoftwareCare. We even discovered an opportunity for SoftwareCare to acquire a French player who was well established in the European market.

CASE STUDY 8: DevFast – Evaluating levels of market interest for a new technology

Business Profile

Company Name: DevFast (start-up)

Industry: Advanced manufacturing

DevFast develops materials technologies that can be utilised within several sectors, including energy, chemicals, environment and health.

Past Business Activities

DevFast had developed a breakthrough technology which could potentially revolutionise a specific industry sector.

Major Challenges

The main challenge for DevFast was being able to test and confirm that the development of their technology was heading to the right direction. To achieve this aim, they had to gather feedback from a large European company. They had clearly identified the company they wanted to target – a major industry player worldwide. They wanted a fast introduction to this company's head of R&D because Gary (one of the owners of DevFast) was travelling to Europe soon.

How Exportia Helped

Our team at Exportia quickly identified the head of R&D of the European company. We contacted them, requesting an appointment, which we obtained easily as we had clearly outlined the agenda of Gary's meeting to them.

We also invited one of our Europe team members based in the region to participate in the meeting and provide support for any language and business-related issues.

Final Outcome

The meeting with the key contact person was secured on time. The outcome for DevFast was mainly to be able to determine the direction of future development of this technology based on feedback from a market leader.

CASE STUDY 9: FastProtect – Establishing a network of sales agents in a specific European market

Business Profile

Company Name: FastProtect (small business)
Industry: Advanced manufacturing

FastProtect manufactures an electronic device used in a broad range of industries, including construction and mining.

Past Business Activities

Exportia had previously assisted FastProtect to establish their distribution within a European country. The European distributor's sales representatives now required some support in order to really kick-start sales.

Main Challenges

The main challenge was that the product was new in the market and quite groundbreaking. Even though the product is fairly easy to demonstrate and understand, the sales rep needed to have confidence to be able to instruct others in its use. At this point, the distributors' sales representatives had more incentive to sell competitive products that are manufactured by market leaders rather than 'cutting their teeth' on a new product.

How Exportia Helped

Initially, Exportia identified the best sales agents by interviewing distributors, agents, and other manufacturers. Once we'd found an agent who complied with FastProtect's criteria, we set up a Skype interview between them and Roger, the Australian CEO and Janette, the product manager. The objective of the Skype call was for Roger and Janette to be comfortable with the agent's profile, including their skills and mindset. For the agent, it was a way of clarifying the commission on sales terms and payment terms. Once Roger, Janette and I were happy with the interview, we asked the agent for three referrals. The Exportia team then contacted the three referrals and, in parallel, we asked them to send us their contract for review. When FastProtect was happy with the contract and the feedback, we then confirmed with the agent and organised signatures. We also organised training, demo kits and brochures to enable the agent to start working with the company. We also organised a conference call with a French lawyer so that Roger would have a full understanding of the terms of French sales agents' contracts.

Final Outcome

We appointed a network of five hand-picked sales agents in different regions, thereby providing support for the distributors' sales representatives for product training, technical questions, sales calls and during marketing events. This network covered the majority of France.

CASE STUDY 10: FlowForecast – Determining European countries with most potential for a specific technology

Business Profile

Company Name: FlowForecast (start-up)

Industry: Cleantech, IT

FlowForecast has developed a software tool to conduct on-demand forecasting for utilities companies.

Past Business Activities

FlowForecast had established commercial activities in the Australian market and wanted to 'dip their toes in the European waters'.

Major Challenges

Being a start-up, FlowForecast had limited financial and human resources and did not know where to start. They wanted to ensure that they focused on the European country or countries which had the most potential for their business.

FlowForecast as keen to get an indication of the level of interest for their technology by understanding the business problems that European utilities operators often face, and whether their software tool could help solve them. They also wanted to find out if there was any government incentive that might encourage the purchase of their technology.

How Exportia Helped

The Exportia team contacted managers in charge of forecasting for three to five utilities operators in three different European markets. We then interviewed each of them about the regulations in their country, the type of tools they were currently using and their level of satisfaction with them.

Final Outcome

Exportia identified which country offered the best opportunities for the software solution and had the least competitive products already established. We also recommended a specific country which was home to the largest multinationals in the industry sector targeted by FlowForecast.

In addition, we guided FlowForecast to successfully enrol in, and be part of, one of the multinational company's programs designed specifically for start-ups, which helped to significantly raised their profile.

NEXT STEPS

Having now read this book, you're potentially at the start of an exciting journey. For any high-tech business, exporting to Europe has the potential to absolutely transform your company. It continually brings up new challenges for you and it can lead you to completely revamp your business model. What I continually find with my Australian clients is that exporting goes beyond just selling overseas; it helps them to secure new investors and de-risk their business, as well as encouraging them to innovate. Furthermore, it engages their whole staff on a journey that causes them to develop and grow.

This is why I'm passionate about what I do. I love making a contribution to the lives of business owners and seeing the impact of what we can do for their company: whether it's new jobs, new product development, new investors coming on board, or witnessing them winning export awards. This is exactly the reason why I founded Exportia in 2006.

Every day, my team and I work with very smart CEOs who challenge us and push us to achieve the best possible exporting outcomes for their business. At the same time, we provide guidance and the essential information they need to make the best decisions for their company. This is why I designed the 'GoToEurope program' to secure every step towards success for high-tech businesses wanting to export to Europe. As one of my CEO clients told me recently, when a small business wants to export, it gambles time and money. So, by deciding to work with Exportia, business owners have control and gain knowledge of exactly what their European clients want and what they have to do to meet their needs. They also get clarity with regards to the next steps needed to improve their current situation, overcome obstacles and open up new markets and opportunities.

Over the years, I have worked with many different CEOs and small businesses in the technology sector and, as a result, I have developed a framework that sets out the necessary steps and the major milestones required to become a successful exporter to Europe. I call my exporting framework the Exportia 'GoToEurope program' and it is based on my previous successes and what has worked for my clients.

Are you serious about breaking into the European market but are finding it hard to know where to start? Or are you already active in the European market but want to take it a step further? If so, please feel free to get in touch with me and my team at Exportia.

You can email me at readytechgo@exportia.com.au to discuss where your business is currently and how Exportia can assist you. If you don't know where to start, have a particular issue you want to solve regarding the European market, or you just need some initial information about exporting, we are always happy to help.

To help you to decide if your business is ready to consider exporting to Europe, we can offer you an 'Exportia GO360' evaluation session. In the preparatory stages, when you are thinking about launching into the European marketplace, following these important steps will help you to achieve your exporting goals. The good news is that if you send us an email with the code #ReadyTechGo you can claim a free 'Exportia GO360' evaluation session.

GUEST SPEAKER

Over the past ten years, Christelle Damiens has conducted a range of workshops and presentations on exporting technology to the European market.

She is available to present on a range of subjects including:
- Becoming export ready
- Exporting in business to business (B2B) environments
- Recruiting, managing and motivating European distributors
- Selecting the right European market for your business
- Exporting technology
- Exporting for small businesses
- Exporting to Europe for the medical device, health, bio-technologies, clean technologies, telecommunications, ICT and/or advanced manufacturing industries.

Christelle's workshops and presentations are designed to:
- inspire entrepreneurs to export to Europe
- work with your small business on your exporting strategy for the European market
- solve any issues you may have already encountered in the European market
- define your direction to accelerate your sales in Europe.

Book a workshop with Christelle today to help take you a step closer to Europe. Booking requests can be emailed to: info@exportia.com.au

ABOUT THE AUTHOR

Christelle Damiens founded Exportia in 2006, shortly after migrating from France to Australia. Prior to this, she worked for six years in sales at IBM Paris. Christelle then made the decision to turn her back on a successful corporate career and return to her passion for international business (with a particular focus on small business). She discovered that her past European sales experience in a high-tech environment, together with her ability to communicate in five languages (English, French, German, Italian and Hindi) meant that she had a lot to offer Australian small and medium enterprises. Christelle understands that Australian SMEs are looking to grow internationally, but they often lack the time and also the financial and human resources to take the next step.

Over the past decade while working closely with dozens of Australian high-tech companies, Christelle has developed a powerful 7-step exporting framework (called the 'GoToEurope program'), as well as a set of online tools tailored specifically to the needs of technology companies to enable them to export successfully to Europe.

Christelle has an MBA from Edith Cowan University in Perth and a degree in business administration from the École de Management de Normandie. She is the managing director of Exportia Australia and the president of Exportia France. Christelle was appointed French foreign trade adviser by the French Prime Minister and served in this role from 2010

till 2013. In 2008, her company was nominated for a Best
Australian Small Business Award in its category.

Christelle lives in Sydney with her family and travels regularly to Europe.

'We engaged Christelle because she understood our market. Most importantly, she has the right set of skills and experience in cross-country transactions. Christelle has the ability to make things happen!'

Anthony Kittel – CEO, Redarc Electronics

'Christelle has unique commercial and interpersonal skills that enable our business to hold discussions with high-level decision makers. Because of her calibre and experience, Christelle has established the right executive engagement with our large enterprise European clients to build the professional relationships needed to compete in this large market.'

Dr Alex Birrell – CEO, Paftec Australia

'Christelle Damiens understood the specifics of our industry very rapidly. She gave us a clear picture of our market; it was really helpful and reassuring to have her support during meetings. She has bridged the gap and made sure that there were no misunderstandings between us and our clients. As a result, we have recently decided to engage the services of Exportia to develop our sales for another product in another industry and it's already looking promising for us.'

Vincent De Sutter – Managing Director, De Sutter Frères

'As a result of engaging with the European headquarters of one of the world's largest train manufacturers, Christelle Damiens from Exportia was able to introduce us to key decision makers at the Australian subsidiary. This resulted in a request for a proposal to participate in a large rail project in Victoria.'

Michael Wilson – Business Development Manager, Chess Engineering

www.ingramcontent.com/pod-product-compliance
Lightning Source LLC
Chambersburg PA
CBHW070359200326
41518CB00011B/1992